I0809861

THE

MAKING OF AMERICA

SERIES

KEYPORT

FROM PLANTATION TO CENTER OF COMMERCE AND INDUSTRY

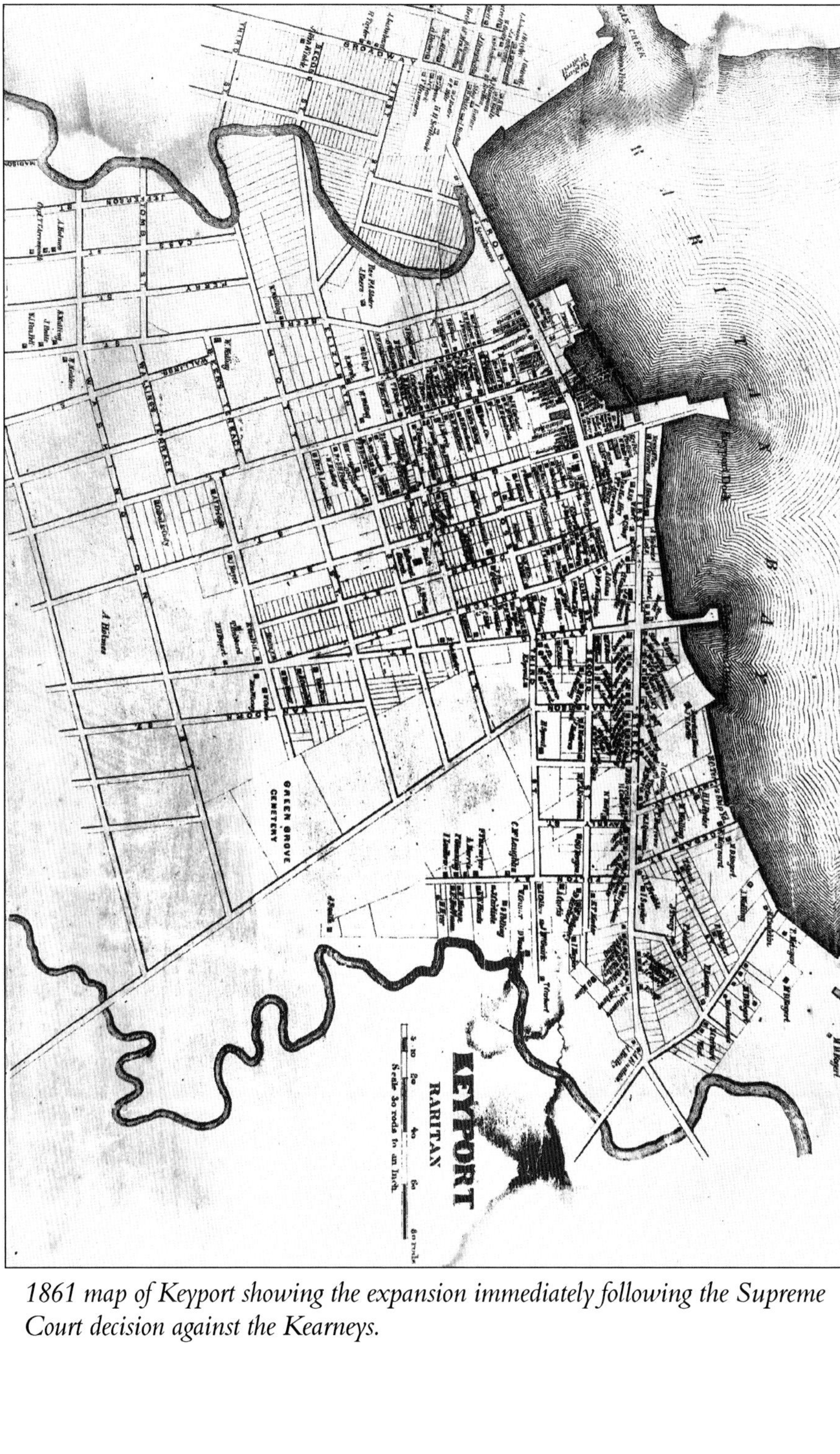

1861 map of Keyport showing the expansion immediately following the Supreme Court decision against the Kearneys.

THE
MAKING OF AMERICA
SERIES

KEYPORT
FROM PLANTATION TO CENTER OF COMMERCE AND INDUSTRY

JACK JEANDRON

ARCADIA
PUBLISHING

ISBN 978-0-7385-2439-9

Published by Arcadia Publishing
Charleston, South Carolina

Printed in the United States of America

Library of Congress Catalog Card Number: 2003106999

For all general information contact Arcadia Publishing at:
Telephone 843-853-2070
Fax 843-853-0044
E-Mail sales@arcadiapublishing.com
For customer service and orders:
Toll-Free 1-888-313-2665

Visit us on the Internet at www.arcadiapublishing.com

Front cover: Oystermen at Keyport waterfront with a full catch aboard.

Contents

ACKNOWLEDGMENTS

I have always been interested in history, and when I joined the Keyport Historical Society I found a good quantity of interesting material about Keyport—my hometown. The chief source was the Keyport Weekly, particularly thanks to the Brown family, who owned and guided it for many years. I decided that the Keyport story needed to be expanded into a book. Many people have helped and influenced me in this endeavor. My wife Angel has provided constant support, ferreting out material, checking details, and always encouraging me. Dallas Swan, nephew of Vincent J. Burnelli, opened the files of Burnelli Corporation to me and confirmed the Chalmers H. Goodlin story of the aborted signing of the B-36 bomber contract. So many others who have provided information include Clyde MacKenzie, Bob Holtz, Dan Kusrow, Wilbur Huylar, Anita Slovenz, Meta Conklin, Al Bennett, Lillian Waterman, Grace Buhler, Dave Baker, and Leon Schanck Jr. Helen Henderson was very helpful in guiding me through the intricacies of dealing with publication. I have Moe and Marge Cuocci both to thank for their zeal in collecting images of Keyport and the Keyport Historical Society for making their images available. Bob Moore stepped in to provide sketches to support the Prohibition chapter where photos were not available. Yvonne Murphy helped by drawing maps. Lester Horner was generous in providing prints of many scenes he captured. And finally, I want to thank those wonderful librarians, Jackie LaPolla and Judy Revere, at the Keyport Library for making research such a pleasure.

INTRODUCTION

This is the history of Keyport, but it also includes the histories of the borough's companies and institutions, which are stories within a story. The aim has been to tell these separate narratives as they relate to one another. Dates are always provided to keep things in perspective. I believe that history should always be factual—never conjectural—and this principle has been followed throughout the book. So many times, I have heard the accusation that Dr. James Philip Kearney was a wastrel or he could not manage his money when circumstantially other conclusions were much more logical. I have presented the facts and left judgment to the readers.

Within the one and a half square mile borders of Keyport, there is a wealth of history. There is much more than can be said that is of interest. For readers looking for more detail or other topics, I can only say the scope had to be kept within bounds. Admittedly, there is some history included outside the territorial bounds of Keyport, such as the expansion of Jersey Central Traction Company beyond Keyport and coverage of Vincent Burnelli before and after Keyport. However, to omit those passages would severely detract from the overall story. I hope the reader will find these pages as interesting to read as they were to write and that these passages will inculcate an appreciation for Keyport—my hometown.

1. The Beginnings

There were many Lenape tribes of Native Americans in and around what is now Keyport. There was also a great deal of foot traffic between the shore (including Keyport) and the more populated areas along the Delaware River to the west, especially during the summer. On early maps of New Jersey, an Indian path is shown running from the mouth of the Shrewsbury River to Middletown; at that point, there were two trails to the Delaware River, one inland path through Spotswood, the other a shore path through Keyport and the Amboys and thence inland through Morristown to Minisink Island on the Delaware. The Keyport shore, including Conasconk Point, was a very popular summer camping area because of the plentiful supply of Chingarora oysters, and it appears there may have been some year-round residence. For many years, there were piles of oyster shells along the shore. Local residents have found arrow and axe heads, and grinding mills in various places throughout the town.

Three Indian deeds cover the section of New Jersey embraced by Monmouth County. They were dated 1665–1666 and duly acknowledged before Governor Nicolls of New York. On April 8, 1666, the Governor signed the "Monmouth Patent." Present at the acknowledgement were 16 Native Americans, 12 white men, and the governor and his executives. Among the white men purchasing the land were John Bowne and Richard Stout.

On March 21, 1664, Charles II gave a patent to his brother, James, Duke of York, for a great part of North America including the provinces of New York and New Jersey and all other lands thereto appertaining with power of government. On June 23 and 24, 1664, the Duke of York granted and conveyed to John, Lord Berkeley, and Sir George Carteret all that tract of land hereinafter to be called Nova Caesarea, or New Jersey.

In 1674, New Jersey was divided into two sections. West New Jersey was sold to Quakers by Lord Berkeley and East New Jersey was retained by Sir George Carteret. On June 20, 1687, the Proprietors of the Province of East New Jersey sold 240 acres to John Bound (Bowne) containing the land now known as Keyport.

Captain John Bound thus became the original Monmouth patentee for this area "who under the Nicolls Patent purchased land of the Indians and after receiving his town lots, located his own plantation with Richard Stout in Pleasant Valley or Chingaroras." The place where he located is the present Township of Holmdel, although in old records he is mentioned as one of the settlers of Middletown, which at the time included this area.

Captain John Bound and his son John purchased from time to time and had patented over 10,000 acres of land situated in Monmouth County and other parts of the state. The northern boundary of the original tract was Raritan Bay, which includes what is now Keyport.

Workers found Indian skeletons when they excavated to lay water pipe on Cedar Street. This and the Indian chiefs' burial ground in Holmdel indicate a more than transitory presence in the area.

2. The Kearney Plantation

On July 21, 1714, John Bowne sold 340 acres of land to Thomas Kearney and Michael Kearney, merchants of New York. The area was bounded by Chingarora Creek on the east, Raritan Bay on the north, Matawan Creek on the west, and Abraham Watson's land (approximately where Clark Street is today) on the south. Included in the purchase were grist and boiling mills, and all materials pertaining to them. On the same date, he also sold them:

> all my whole stock of Swin [swine] great and small and all Neat [head of] Cattle and allsoe my two Cannoes, Planks & timbers, scales, waits, Beams, baggs, measures will [with] all necessary and utensyles belonging to this plantation. My Household goods and Six Hoggs Excepted.

The description of goods sold clearly connotes a fair degree of development (grist and boiling mills and livestock) and the existence of one dwelling. There was an excellent natural harbor with inlets and stands of timber with salt marshes and arable land.

A year and a half later, on November 14, 1715, Thomas Kearney bought his brother Michael's one-third interest in the plantation. The Kearney mansion, on a centrally-located knoll overlooking the bay called Wolf Pit Hill, was completed in 1717. Thomas and Catherine Kearney and their five children moved in 1717 to their new home, which they named Key Grove Farm or Plantation after their ancestral home in Ireland. In the years from then to 1807, the plantation grew to a total of 1,000 acres.

Old deeds and records show that Thomas Kearney Sr., his son Captain Thomas Kearney Jr., and his grandson Captain Edmund Kearney were all involved in the coastal shipping industry and their principal cargo was wood of various kinds grown on the Kearney Plantation. In old deeds, mention is made of "well timbered woodland." This included young timber and York-wood, fencing timber and cordwood, timber for wood fire and ship building, and staves. The various tracts of land owned by the Kearneys were all "within fence." One tract had 100 apple trees and also peach, plum, and cherry trees.

Thomas Kearney Sr. was managing owner of two sloops, the *Catherine* and the *Content*. Captain Thomas Kearney Jr. commanded the sloop *Content* for his father. In 1740, Thomas Kearney Sr. presented his son Thomas with half interest in this vessel:

> Know all men by these presents that I, Thomas Kearney of Middletown in the County of Monmouth [the plantation was then part of Middletown], Mer'cht for & in consideration of the natural Love I bear to my Son Thomas Kearney of Sd. Middletown & County aforesaid, have given, granted & made over unto the said Thomas Kearney, jun'r one moyty [moiety] or half part of a certain sloop called the Content with half her sayles & rigging burthen twelve cords or thereabout. To have and to hold the said half part of said sloop & rigging &c, unto the said Thomas Kearney, in & tho heirs of said body for ever and want of such heirs to my son James Kearney. . . . In Witness whereof I have hereunto set my hand and seal this twentyth day of September & thirteenth year of his Maj'ties Reign Annoq Domini, 1740

Thomas Kearney Sr. owned 70 slaves. The bill of sale for his purchase of one of them is as follows:

> Know all men by these presents that I, John Web of the City of Perth Amboy, Merc'ht for and in consideration of the sum of fifteen pounds current money of New Jersey, to me in hand paid by Thomas Kearney

The sloop shown is similar to those owned and operated by the Kearneys.

> of the County of Monmouth, merc'ht. whereof I hereby acknowledge the receipt & myself therewith fully satisfied, have bargained, sold & delivered unto the said Thomas Kearney one Negro man called Hary, aged forty-five years or thereabout to have and to hold the said Negro man unto the said Thomas Kearney, his Exe'rs, Adm'rs, assigns forever. . . . In witness whereof I have hereunto set my hand & seal this 3 day of Dec'r Annoq Domini 1729.

In March 1737, Thomas and Catherine Kearney presented their oldest son John with the Brown's Point section of the plantation, which by this time totaled 510 acres. In August 1742, John Kearney, who had by then re-married, deeded Brown's Point to his father and his brother James. John died four years later and Thomas Kearney Sr. passed on a year later in 1747. He left to his wife Catherine an annuity, furniture, silver, and slaves. His will notes that his son John had received money and slaves.

To his son Thomas Kearney Jr., he left the Key-Grove plantation, which then totaled 750 acres. In his will, he noted that this property had been bought from John Bowne in 1714 and 1715, John Johnstone in 1714, Elisha Lawrence in 1717, Lawrence Smith in 1717, and John and Hannah Willson in 1719. To his son James Kearney, he left his interest in the Brown's Point plantation.

In 1750, Thomas Kearney Jr. married Mrs. Mary Reid Hartshorne, a widow with two children. They in turn had eight of their own, two of whom did not survive early childhood. The Kearney plantation changed with the purchase and sale of adjoining properties. In 1752, Thomas Kearney Jr. sold two tracts of land in the area called "Way Cake" (Waackaack). In 1764, he bought property at Chingaroras at public vendue. Thomas and Mary Kearney lived through stormy times. They continued to run the Kearney plantation and engage in the shipping trade with the sloops *Catherine* and *Content*. Thomas Kearney's son Edmund in time became captain of the *Catherine*.

Beyond this peaceful setting, storms were brewing that would develop into the Revolutionary War. In Boston, patriots dressed as Indians had staged the Boston Tea Party in December 1773. The British, in retaliation, had closed the port of Boston. In 1774, the patriots of Monmouth County freely contributed to the suffering inhabitants of Boston, sending 1,140 bushels of rye and 50 barrels of rye meal. A letter was sent on October 21, 1774, thanking the citizens of Monmouth County for enabling them to oppose the Parliamentary Acts. A Monmouth Tea Party was held in Sandy Hook Bay in April 1775.

Monmouth County suffered more severely than other New Jersey counties through the forays and depredations of bands of loyalists called Tory Refugees. The British Army had established itself on Staten Island. The Tory Refugees had fled to Staten Island for protection and had established an armed camp on Sandy Hook called Refugee Town. This was a convenient base of operations for marauding expeditions against the populace of Monmouth County. Many of the inhabitants, although secretly favoring the American cause, were obliged to feign allegiance to the crown or

Map showing the relationship of Kearney Plantation to locations of British troops on Staten Island and Tory Refugees at Sandy Hook.

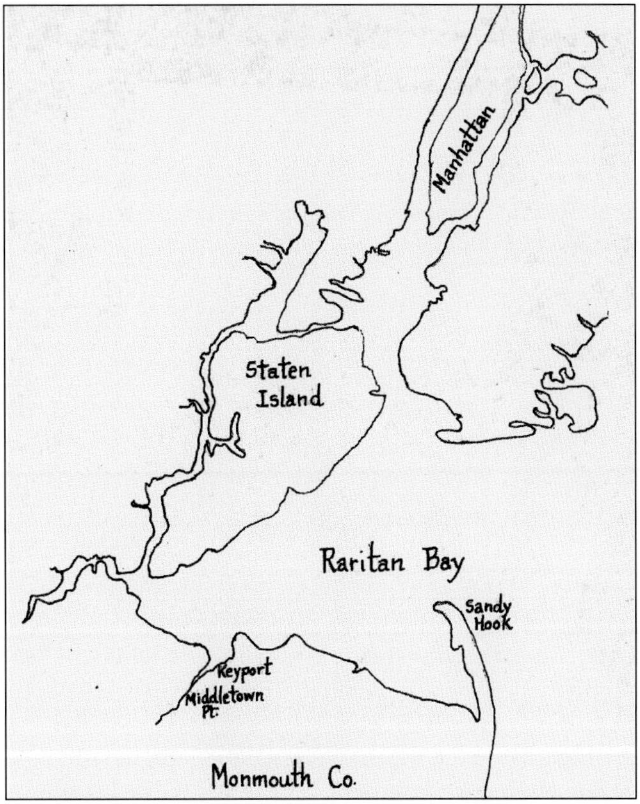

lose their property and possessions to the marauding Tory Refugees. Among those in this situation was Major Thomas Kearney Jr., of Washington's New Jersey militia.

On one occasion, a party of 30 or 40 Refugees stopped at Major Kearney's dwelling on their way to Middletown Point (Matawan), where they intended to burn a dwelling and some mills. Thomas Kearney feigned gratification at their visit and falsely informed them there were probably some rebel troops at the Point, which would present a danger to them. He sent his African-American servant Jube to make inquiries, having previously instructed him how to act. Jube returned to report a massive buildup of rebels about to march toward the Kearney plantation. The Refugees were alarmed and hastily retreated in their boats.

On another occasion in 1780, the Refugees eluded rebel scouts and plundered several houses including that of J. Mott Sr. where they took prisoners, slaves, and stock. On June 3, 1778, there was also a successful foray by a loyalist party which landed near Major Kearney's place and proceeded to Middletown Point. There they captured John Burrowes and burned his mills and stock houses. They also captured several officers in the rebel militia.

During the Revolutionary War, the part of the Kearney plantation bordering the bay and east of Luppatatong Creek was fenced off and called the "Cow Pen Lots." Tory farmers would bring cattle here in the night and British soldiers

Mary Kearney's school house is now the home of Nola Waterman.

would row over from Staten Island in flat boats or scows to pick them up. Some were provided through loyalty and some through fear that all cattle would be stolen and farms destroyed. For those who cooperated, the British paid in gold. This was the prevailing situation through the American victory at Yorktown. This, of course, was followed by the Treaty of Paris in 1783 and the end of the war.

At the Kearney plantation, matters much more mundane took precedence. On April 7, 1791, Thomas Kearney Jr. deeded Key Grove plantation to his oldest son James for "the Natural love and affection which he hath and beareth to his said son, James Kearney, and also for divers other Causes and Considerations." The other "Causes and Considerations" were that Thomas Kearney Jr., his wife, and his daughter Mary "while she remained unMaryed" were to have life rights to the plantation. Thomas Kearney Jr., at the time, was approximately 90 years old. Mary Kearney was then 24. In a will dated July 16, 1792, Thomas Kearney Jr. bequeathed to his sons Edmund and Phillip properties that would eventually form the greater part of Union Beach. He left to James (who had already been deeded the plantation) two yoke of oxen. To his wife Mary he bequeathed all of his slaves, and to his daughters Euphenia and Mary £100 each.

James Kearney never married. At 60 and ailing away from home in Richmond County, New York, he drew up his will leaving Key Grove Plantation to his brother Edmund. He also bequeathed to him lands purchased from William Baily near Chingaroras Point (Conaskonk Point, Union Beach). All other possessions were bestowed upon Edmund Kearney with the exception of £200 given to his sister Mary and £25 per year to his sister Euphemia. Of importance for events transpiring later, his will also provided that Mary:

> shall be entitled to the full possession and use of two rooms (including one fire place and fire wood) and such use of the cellar and kitchen as she may require in my present dwelling house on Key Grove farm above named; and that these privileges together with that of maintaining five cows and a horse and chair on and with the products of Key Grove farm she shall possess during her natural life.

James Kearney died on January 17, 1811, two days after drawing up his will. In April, Edmund Kearney moved to Key Grove farm, then covering 781 acres. He was married to Ann Bowne and had five children. The farm was described as being divided into many fields and pastures all included by an exterior boundary fence. A part of the estate was fine arable land, but the greater section was covered with a heavy growth of valuable timber. Apparently almost a century of lumbering had not significantly depleted the forest resources of Key Grove farm. There were no roads except by-roads with bars.

Captain Edmund Kearney had been educated in England and was a friend of Horatio Nelson, thus he named one of his sons after him. He was even offered command of a British frigate during the War of 1812 but refused vigorously.

There were two dwellings on Key Grove farm, the mansion and a tenant house (noted above), which is still standing on Snyder Lane. The family burial vault was located near what is now the northwest corner of Perry and Francis Streets. The plot on which it stood was supposed to have been excepted from all deeds, but today there is no trace of the vault. Plaques from it are in the Josephine Brown collection at the library of the Monmouth County Historical Association. There is conjecture that the Kearneys in the vault were re-interred in Perth Amboy in the graveyard of the Episcopal Church. There was a small building near the Kearney mansion used as a schoolhouse that was moved to what is now Kearney Street and is now the residence of Nola Waterman. Since the Kearneys had as many as 70 slaves, there were most likely slave quarters, but their location is unknown.

Most travel in those days was by boat. Roads were almost non-existent. Since there were no roads leading to Key Grove farm or Browns Point in 1829, a petition for a public road was presented to the Superior Court of Common Pleas of the County of Monmouth. The surveyors of Middletown, Freehold, and Shrewsbury were ordered to meet at the house of Septimus Stevens on Browns Point on February 1830. As a result, three roads were laid out including the present Main Street, and the Key Grove area was connected with Middletown and Middletown Point. This development tended to increase the value of the area.

Although this put less demand on the water as a means of transportation, it remained a major resource for sustenance as oysters were planted in the creek all during the days of the Kearneys. William W. Forman lived on Key Grove farm from 1823 to 1828 and planted the shellfish there.

It would not be correct to assume that the area where the Key Grove farm was located was all farm and woodlands. Within 5 miles there were more than a half dozen grist and sawmills. Furthermore, the original purchase from John Bowne included a gristmill, and acquisition was made by the Kearneys in 1717 of a sawmill from Richard Salter. In the article "The Old Mills of Monmouth County," Captain Charles B. Parsons of Red Bank read before the Monmouth County Historical Association in 1912 observations about local mills. In regard to the Thomas Arrowsmith mill (where the Waackaack is crossed by Middle Road), he states:

> Every farm in the locality at that time produced some wheat, rye, corn, oats, and buckwheat, but generally only enough of these for home

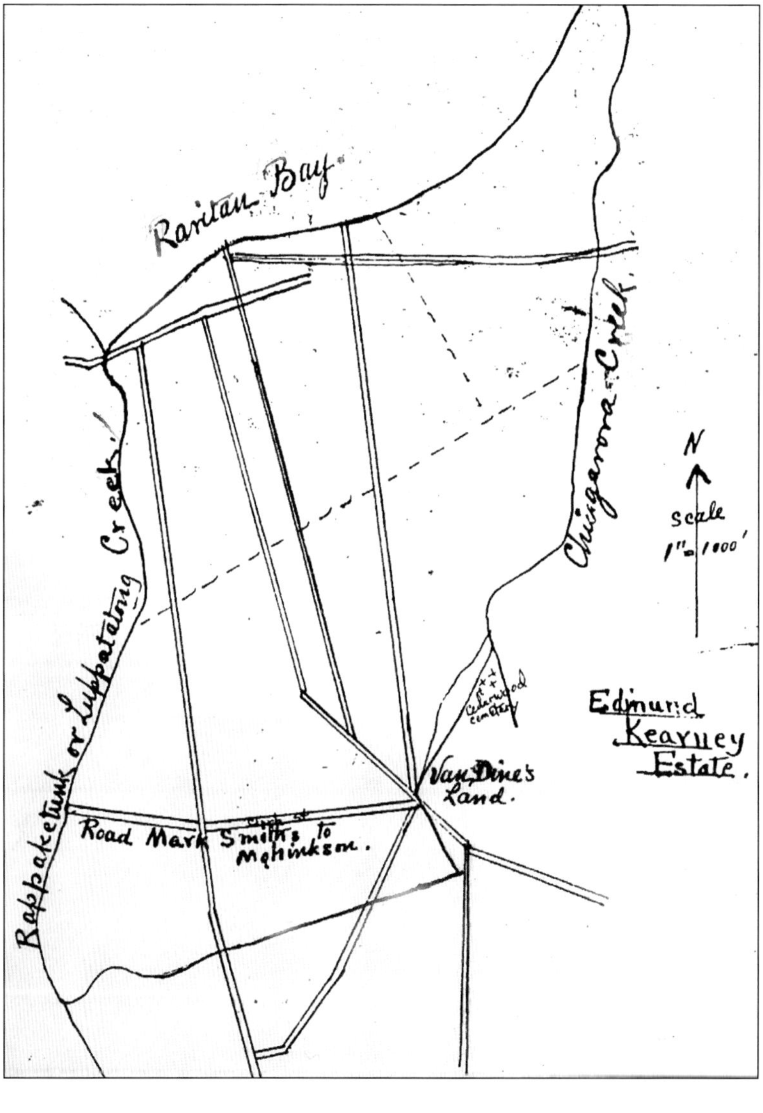

Map of the Edmund Kearney estate.

> consumption. When necessary, a grist, as it was called, was made up of each kind of grain according to the needs of the family and the stock and taken to the mill with instructions to the miller on how it was to be prepared or ground. The result was wheat flour, rye flour, middlings, bran and corn meal, buckwheat flour, hulls, and feed. Rye flour was used principally by most families; wheat flour was used only for special occasions in bread, such as on Sunday, for company, or for hot tea biscuits and pastry; rye bread was the standard for every day use, with corn bread for breakfast, varied by buckwheat cakes and mush made from corn meal.
>
> This mill was one of the largest in the county and enjoyed a good supply of water power, connected with which was a saw mill.
>
> Wallings' mill, which is located on the Middle road, two miles south-east of Keyport [actually between Middle Road and the present Highway 36 near the present Union Avenue], was built in 1705 and was first owned by a Mr. Kovenhoven, now spelled Conover. It was subsequently owned by Philip Briggs, Richard Walling, and his son Taylor Walling. The gristmill had two run of stone, one for flour and one for feed; there was also a sawmill in connection with it. The pond is of moderate size and is supplied by two brooks: one called Pole Brook and the other Chingarora [Chingarora is probably inaccurate]. The power is an over-shot bucket wheel. . . . The Lufburrow mill was located about one mile south of Chapel Hill, which was built and owned by the Lufburrow family for several generations.

This mill ceased operation in 1880 and stood idle until 1910, when it was torn down. At the time saw mills were erected, the area was more forest than cultivated land. When a building was to be erected, larger parts of the frame were hewn out in the woods, and logs for the joists, planks, and boards were taken to the local saw mills.

The Bedle gristmill was built by Thomas Bedle Jr. before 1800. It was located on the upper Luppatatong Creek about 2 miles south of the town (near the Bedle home on Bedle Road in Hazlet). Before 1829, Thomas Bedle partnered with his son Richard and operated the mill for many years until he died in 1847. One of the millstones rolled into the pond and the other was placed as a step before the front door of the farm house. Again, Parsons states:

> Irwins mill was originally owned by the Stout family. In about 1855, it was sold to Mr. Wood, who came from Staten Island, and by him to Mr. Thomas Irwin. This was a gristmill and sawmill combined, about one mile south of Arrowsmith's, and located on the same stream of water [near present Highway 35 between Palmer and Laurel Avenues]. It had a small pond and was able during the summer dry season to run but a portion of the time. . . . The mill was abandoned in 1898.

The *Keyport Weekly* of May 2, 1930, from which the information in this section is drawn, quotes an important conversation for a chapter dealing with the Kearneys:

> Mr. Peter Stout, an elderly resident of the borough, while in conversation with Mr. E. D. Petteys, a former editor of The Keyport Weekly, January 8, 1887, said that he was brought up at Irwin's mill, which was then owned and operated by his father, Peter Stout Sr., and that he remembered distinctly when the site of Keyport was used as farming land and when it belonged to the Kearneys, who used to send their hands to his father's mill with logs to be cut up into lumber, and previous to the laying out of the road, February 1830, now termed Main Street, the farmers who carried produce to the boat, which landed at Brown's Point at a point near where Cuttrell's ways are now located (1887) [the tip of Brown's Point], were compelled to take the road from Mechanicsville to Oak Shades as far as Joseph Bailey's corner and thence to follow Beers Street to a point where it comes out near Burrowes' store and in order to get to Brown's Point the farmers had to ford Luppatatong Creek, where the bridge is now located [now Maple Place causeway].

Cornelius Ackerson came from Warwick, New York, to Monmouth County early in 1800. Some years later, he built a mill on his property "between Burnham's corner and the present Lloyd Road." He operated the mill for about 25 years. Then when Keyport was established as a community, he moved into town and started a wheelwright business. John Burrowes Sr., called the "Corn King," had mills located on Matawan Creek at Middletown Point. On June 3, 1778, he was taken prisoner in a Tory raid, and his mills and storehouses were destroyed.

The *Keyport Weekly* of May 20, 1927, describes what was perhaps the most novel mill of all. From about 1775 to about 1850, a Mr. Van Brakle operated a gristmill at Middlesex Street on Matawan Creek in Middletown Point. Its power derived from the ebb and flow of the tide. A large wheel was rigged in the stream and wide paddles were fastened to it. As the tide rose and fell, the paddles actuated the millstones. These are just a few of the examples of several mills, as an account book of Jonathan Foreman dated April 29, 1729, lists 32 gristmills and/or sawmills in Monmouth County.

At the Kearney Plantation, a separate plantation had been formed at Browns Point. Another James Kearney, Major James Kearney (uncle of the James Kearney who died in 1811) had acquired the Brown's Point tract through purchase from his brother John and inheritance from his father Thomas Kearney Sr. James lived on this tract for the rest of his life and his large and elegant house burned down in May 1772. He immediately rebuilt the homestead house, but not on the palatial scale of the original one. A year later James died.

The mill shown is representative of those found on and around the Kearney Plantation.

James Kearney's first wife was Margaret Reid of Freehold. After she died on March 17, 1770, he married Agnes (Watson) Freneau, widow of Pierre Freneau and mother of Philip Freneau, the poet of the Revolution. Both of Agnes Watson Freneau Kearney's husbands were buried in the Kearney vault at Key Grove. She never re-married and died October 13, 1817, at the age of 91.

James Kearney and his first wife Margaret had five daughters living at the time of his death, who inherited Brown's Point tract. He and his second wife Agnes had no children. Major Kearney had surveyed and laid out the broad highway (now called Broadway) through his plot of land, leading to the wharf on Raritan Bay. The shipping industry was a thriving one, and the dock was used extensively by farmers in the vicinity to ship their produce to the New York market.

In old deeds, we find that James Kearney and his first wife deeded to Alexander Van Pelt a tract of land at Brown's Point on April 6, 1755. We also find that he sold land to William Smith, Winant Bennet, William Leguear, and others. Winant Bennet, in turn, sold property to Jacobus "Cobus" Morrell and Walter Van Pelt; Van Pelt then sold his land to Morrell in 1794. He established the Brown's Point Tavern House on this property, which was also a hotel for the accommodation of the public. He married Mary Brown, and they had five children—all born in the Tavern House. He died at the age of 49 years. Mrs. Morrell married Septimus Stevens in 1819 and soon the establishment came to be known as Septimus Stevens's Tavern. It was at this site that the Orphan's Court sale of Key Grove

Plantation took place in 1829. The files of the Monmouth County Historical Association show that there was a second hotel on Brown's Point. A tavern license for "keeping a public house of entertainment" and providing lodging and livery service at Brown's Point was issued to "Josep" Holmes for continuing such service in 1798 and 1799.

All history of the Kearney era states that on the Key Grove farm there were only two dwellings: the mansion on Wolf Pit Hill and the tenant farmer house in what is now the Lockport section of Keyport. There is evidence, however, that there were additional dwellings. The Kearneys kept as many as 70 slaves on their plantation. The number fluctuated, but slaves had to be housed no matter how rudimentary their dwellings may have been.

In addition, in the house the author owns at 80 Main Street, a tombstone was used as part of the footing for one of the central columns of the house. The house was built in 1854, but the tombstone (for Leonard Carhart, age 5) is dated 1827—while the Kearneys still owned Key Grove plantation. The other materials were brought in, but why would a tombstone be brought in for building material?

By the time of Edmund Kearney's death in 1822, the Kearneys had lived at Key Grove plantation for over a century. It appeared that a dynasty had been established that would last for centuries. However, Edmund Kearney's death heralded cataclysmic events that would change a sprawling plantation into a thriving town.

Major James Kearney's homestead. It was built to replace a larger structure that burned in 1772.

3. Keyport Emerges

Edmund Kearney died December 30, 1822. Since he left no will, his estate was divided equally among his seven children. The children with their birth dates were: James Phillip—December 1801, Horatio—October 1803, Mary Eliza— November 1808, Thomas—September 1810, Anastasia—October 1813, Catherine—June 1816, and Anne—June 1818. (According to Stillwell, Thomas and Mary were twins, but per Mary's testimony at the later trial, they were not.)

On December 31, 1822, one day after his father's death, James Phillip came of age, while the remaining children were minors. Joseph Taylor was appointed guardian for the minor children. James Phillip Kearney had been studying medicine and in October 1823 was licensed by Censors to practice medicine. It should be noted that in the years 1820 to 1822 the United States was in the throes of a serious economic depression following the panic of 1819. Even the great cotton planters of the south were in serious trouble. Merchants like the Kearneys had been inundated with paper money issued by state banks that failed when the Second Bank of the United States demanded payment of the paper money in specie.

Dr. James Phillip Kearney borrowed $400 from his uncle William W. Forman on December 23, 1823, using his one-seventh interest in the estate as collateral. He was then admitted to the Monmouth County Medical Society in April 1824. He moved to Upper Freehold, where he practiced medicine. It appears he rented quarters, because there is no record of his owning property. On May 5, 1828, he sold his interest in the Key Grove Plantation to John and Daniel W. Holmes for $1,600 subject to a lien to the estate of William W. Forman (his uncle had died) and the life rights of James Phillip's aunt, Mary Kearney. He was practicing medicine in a rural area in difficult times. It might logically be assumed that the funds were necessary for him to maintain a practice. Between May and October 1828, however, Dr. James Phillip Kearney died. The inventory of his estate, dated October 28, 1828, shows a remainder of money due from Daniel and John Holmes of $582.78 and sundry accounts due of $426.14 included in the net worth of his estate of $1,182.67. He did not live long enough to collect all of the $1,600 for his one-seventh interest.

In the April term of 1829 of the Orphan's Court of Monmouth, Daniel Holmes applied for himself and John W. Holmes a petition for an order of partition of the Kearney Estate for severance of their one-seventh share. Only Horatio Kearney was of age at this point, and James Phillip was dead. The court appointed three commissioners as disinterested persons to survey the property and make a division of it to satisfy the claim of John and Daniel Holmes. The commissioners appointed were: James Hopping, Captain Edward Taylor, and Leonard Walling. They surveyed the property, presented a map, and declared that:

> We have caused a survey and map or draught of the premises to be made, and after viewing the same are of the opinion that the said premises are so circumstanced that a division thereof cannot be made without great prejudice to the interests of the owners.

The Court then ordered the Commissioners to sell the entire estate at auction. The subsequent sale divided the estate (which could not be divided without prejudice) into 15 lots for auction, including one containing the home where the Kearney orphans lived. On September 1, 1829, to publicize the sale, the following announcement was posted throughout the County:

> In pursuance of an order of the Orphan's Court of the County of Monmouth, in the term of July 1829, will be exposed to sale and public vendue, on Tuesday the 3rd of November next, on the premises, all that farm at Key Grove in the Township of Middletown, in said County, late the property of Edmund Kearney, deceased, containing 781 acres, 350 of which is woodland, the residue arable land and meadow; on said farm is a good two story Dwelling House with a kitchen adjoining, an excellent Barn, Wagon House and other out buildings; an apple orchard and a variety of other fruit trees. The location of said farm which is on the easterly side of and adjoining to Brown's Point Cove, which is the best harbor on Raritan Bay between Sandy Hook and South Amboy, the small expense for which docks and piers may be built on the same, which vessels could come to and go from, at almost any time of tide, the small expense for which wood may be put on board of vessels, the certainty of its becoming the place of exportation for the greater part of the produce of the county, if properly managed. The advantage of cultivating oysters in Rapatoting Creek which belongs to said farm, and the quality of the soil, which may be so well adapted to the growth of market truck, makes it a most desirable property – for the speculator, the capitalist, and the agriculturist that can be offered in the County of Monmouth, said farm will be divided into several lots or tracts—and sold separately or altogether as may best suit purchasers.
>
> Vendue to commence, at 12 o'clock, noon, and continue from day to day till all is sold, where attendance will be given and conditions made known by.

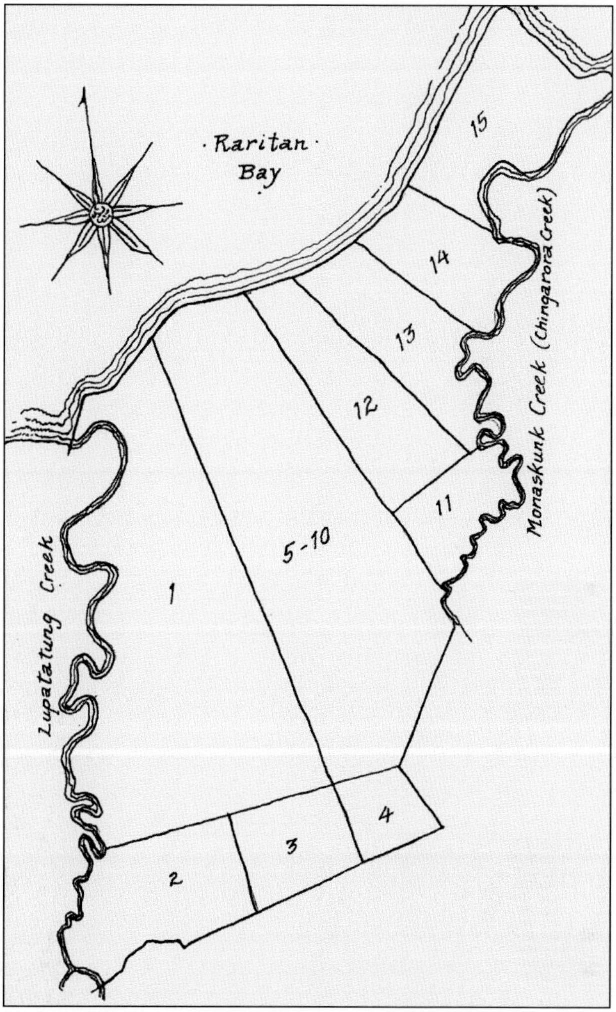

The division of the Kearney Plantation into 15 lots for the Orphan's Court sale.

The auction started on November 3, 1829, at Septimus Stevens's Tavern in Brown's Point with the sale of lot number 1 containing the mansion house. According to testimony presented at the subsequent suit, Daniel Holmes suggested to Richard Burrowes that he and others buy Fishing Point (lot number 8, the prime waterfront area for erecting a dock). Rumor had it that Joseph Ellis and others from Middletown Point were interested in buying Lot number 8 to prevent improvements and avoid competition with their facilities at Middletown Point. Other testimony presented at the later suit denied any interest by Joseph Ellis and the others. Sale of all 15 lots was made to the following purchasers:

Lot no. 1—224.82 acres—Isaac Lippincott
Lot no. 2—56.42 acres—Thomas Carhart

Lot no. 3—32.85 acres—Amos Walling
Lot no. 4—18.43 acres—Jonathan Tilton
Lot no. 5—59.52 acres—Ezra Osborn
Lot no. 6—56.24 acres—Ezra Osborn
Lot no. 7—48.46 acres—Isaac K. Lippincott
Lot no. 8—24.11 acres—Richard C. Burrowes
[actually a company of eight people]
Lot no. 9—7.34 acres—Isaac K. Lippincott
Lot no. 10—16.51 acres—Ezra Osborn
Lot no. 11—59.13 acres—James Sproul
Lot no. 12—26.02 acres—Thomas J. Walling
Lot no. 13—49.42 acres—Amos Walling
Lot no. 14—40.35 acres—Joseph Carhart
Lot no. 15—61.34 acres—Horatio Kearney

The company of eight bidding on Lot number 8 were Isaac Lippincott, Richard Burrowes, Horatio Kearney, Ezra Osborn, Septimus Stevens (who later withdrew), Primrose Hopping, John Hopping, and Daniel Holmes. Daniel Holmes, Richard Burrowes, and Horatio Kearney sold their interests for $40 advance to Joseph Taylor, John Taylor, and David Bray, respectively. The final composition of the

The Nimrod Bedle home on Main Street. The right side was the first house built after Key Port was established; the rest of the house was added later.

company following the sale was: Joseph Taylor, John I. Taylor, David S. Bray, Ezra Osborn, Isaac Lippincott, and Leonard Walling, each holding a one-eighth share, and John Hopping, James Hopping, and Primrose Hopping together holding two one-eighth shares.

The participation of Horatio Kearney, the only one of the living Kearneys who was over 21, is subject to speculation. He was the purchaser of Lot number 15 and was one of the company of eight. In both cases he sold to David S. Bray. At the age of 26 and not having received funds from his share of the estate, his source to make such large purchases for the times is a curious anomaly.

It was noted in the subsequent trial that most of the purchases of lots were related to either Leonard Walling, the Orphan's Court appointed commissioner, or Joseph Taylor, the orphans' guardian and administrator of the estate. The interrelationships are as follows:

Thomas Carhart (purchaser lots 2 and 14)—cousin of Leonard Walling
Amos Walling (purchaser lots 3 and 13)—cousin of Leonard Walling
Ezra Osborn (purchaser lots 5, 6, and 10—son-in-law of Joseph Taylor
Richard C. Burrowes (purchaser lot 8)—son-in-law of Joseph Taylor
James Sproul (purchaser lot 11)—related to Joseph Taylor's wife
Thomas J. Walling (purchaser lot 12)—cousin of Leonard Walling
Jonathan Tilton (purchaser lot 4)—did not take deed. Deed executed to Joseph R. Walling—cousin or brother of Leonard Walling Deeds to lots 5, 6, 7, 8, 9, 10 (purchased by Osborn, Burrowes, & Lippincott) were executed to John I. Taylor—son of Joseph Taylor
Deed to lot 11 (purchased by James Sproul) executed to James, John, & Joseph Sproul—brothers-in-law of Joseph Taylor
Deed to lot 13 (purchased by Amos Walling) executed to Amos & William Walling—both cousins of Leonard Walling and to Douglas Stout a connection of Joseph Taylor's wife
James Hopping, who held a part share in the company of eight—also a commissioner
Isaac Lippincott and Horatio Kearney were the only ones not related or connected.

The 15 lots sold at the Orphans' Court sale brought a total of $19,941.19, which was payable to the children and to John and Daniel Holmes for their one-seventh share. The deeds issued as a result of the sale were dated April 1, 1830. One half of the payment for each lot was made following the sale and the other half was payable on April 1, 1830. Lots 5 through 10 were all conveyed to John I. Taylor, who paid the commissioners $4,683.16.

On April 7, 1830, Mary Kearney sold her life rights to the Key Grove Plantation to the new owners for $500. As stated in the previous chapter, she had been given life rights to not only the homestead, but also use of the land. The inventory of Edmund Kearney's estate showed a note from his sister Mary for $118.81. Since in April 1830 she was 62 and unmarried, her ability to repay her debt to the estate (to guardian Joseph Taylor) was extremely limited. Mary Kearney had taught the children and a few neighbors during Edmund Kearney's tenure. It is not known whether she continued to instruct, but teachers in those years were paid the merest pittance for their labors.

Isaac K. Lippincott of Freehold, New Jersey, was the purchaser of Lot number 1 containing the plantation house. Oysters had been cultivated in Luppatatong Creek, and he could see the financial advantages of expanding the oyster beds. In addition, the quality of the soil was well adapted to grow vegetables for market.

In 1830, the Keyport Company built a dock and large storehouse at a cost of $2,000. Leonard Walling supervised the work. He and James Hopping supervised building the first sloop, named the *New Jersey*, in the summer of 1830 at Compton's Creek [now Port Monmouth] at the yards of Francis and John Cuttrell. With James Hopping as captain, it was put in service to ship produce and passengers between New York and the new town. The sloop *Middletown* was built in 1836, and more vessels were added as business increased.

On or about April 9, 1830, the Keyport Company had Leonard Walling survey and plot out 24 building lots. One was kept for a tavern to be erected by the company, and the rest were put up for sale at $25 each. In the spring of 1831, at the suggestion of Leonard Walling, the new town was called Key Port, because it was now a port on the site of the Key Grove plantation. However, the name was somewhat academic, since it was still part of Middletown Township.

By the close of the 1830s, storms were brewing for Key Port. How much advance knowledge there was of coming legal action is not known. However, in 1839 Oliver Vanderbilt, a newcomer to the area, bought the Keyport Company land, dock, and holdings for $7,000.

On August 12, 1840, the commissioners (James Hopping, Edward Taylor, and Leonard Walling) gave permission for Ezra Osborn, Isaac Lippincott, John I. Taylor, Daniel Holmes, David Bray, John Hopping, James Hopping, and Leonard Walling to enter lots 5 through 10 to cut down timber and sell it. In the fall of 1840, George Sullivan, esquire, who was the attorney for the Kearney heirs, contended that there was a flaw in the title from the Orphans' Court sale. The basis for the allegation was that the order of the court was made to one set of persons and the deeds were executed to others. Accordingly, in the fall session of 1840 the Kearney heirs brought suit against the lot owners in the United States Circuit Court. In 1841, Oliver Vanderbilt conveyed portions of the Keyport Company property to John C. Schenck ($205), William R. Jacques ($1,000), David Warner ($375), and John C. Schenck ($6,000).

Testimony at the trial by Isaac Lippincott in 1841 indicated that improvements on the property consisted of about 70 dwellings, two stores, one good public house, two docks, 10 or 12 mechanics' shops, and other buildings. At this point, there were 100 owners of properties, most of whom purchased since the court sale. A considerable portion were persons of small property with their capital completely invested therein. By 1843, improvements to the lots amounted to a value of $100,000, of which $60,000 applied to lots 5 through 10.

In 1843, Thomas Kearney, Catherine Kearney, Anastasia Kearney Thomas, and her husband George C. Thomas sold their interest in the Key Grove property (still under litigation) to Anne E. Kearney. Through the rest of the 1840s, development of the new town slowed to almost nothing.

In 1844, action was taken by the New Jersey legislature. On February 14, 1844, "An Act to Confirm the Sales of Real Estate Whereof Edmund Kearney, Deceased, Late of the County of Monmouth, Died Seized [without a will]" was passed by the Legislative Council and the General Assembly of the state of New Jersey.
In 1848, Raritan Township [currently Hazlet] was established through division of Middletown township, which included Key Port.

In 1851, the court decreed against the heirs. The decision was appealed to the United States Supreme Court and, in 1853, it upheld the decision of the lower court. Thus ended for all time the Kearney claims to the burgeoning new town. The suit was based on the narrow basis of flaw in title as described above. The Orphans' Court decision not to divide the plantation for severance of the Holmes brothers one-seventh share but to divide the entire plantation for auction sale did not enter into the suit, nor did the acquisition of the entire tract by Commissioner Walling, Orphans' Guardian and Administrator Taylor, and their relatives even though the commissioners and guardian were supposed to be disinterested parties.

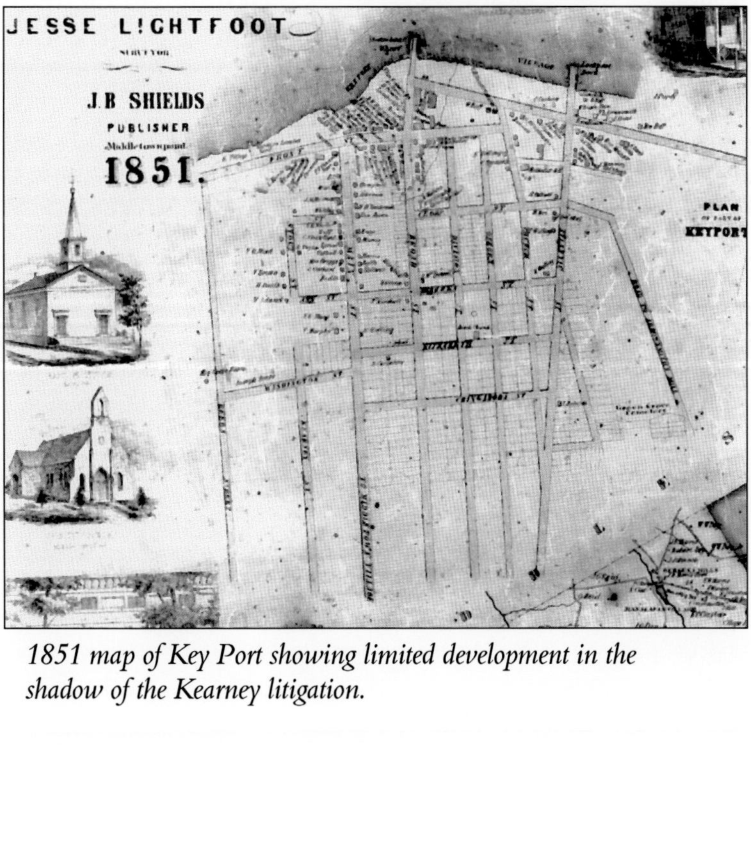

1851 map of Key Port showing limited development in the shadow of the Kearney litigation.

4. Eye of the Needle: Shipping Through Keyport

Following the Orphan's Court sale, as stated in chapter 3, the new owners built a dock and started a shipping company. At first, the business ran sloops; the *New Jersey* of 50 tons was built and put into service in 1832. This operation was to become for Monmouth County the eye of the needle, the port through which most of their commerce flowed.

The *Wave* was the first steamboat to run from Keyport in 1840. The *Inquirer* of September 11, 1845, said that there were now several steamboats running to New York daily: one from Middletown Point, two from Keyport, one from Red Bank, and one from Eatontown. The *Telegraph* with Captain J.T. Weeks ran from Keyport and Middletown Point, and the steam freighting boat *Rockland* with Captain T.V. Arrowsmith and the steamboat *Washington Irving* ran from Keyport. There was traffic out of Middletown Point until about 1847. The shallow creek was a problem, however, so the steamboat companies in the two towns consolidated to form the Keyport & Middletown Point Steamboat Company, which was incorporated in 1852. After 1847, the steamboats ran only from Keyport. The original Keyport Company had been sold to Oliver Vanderbilt of Castleton, New York, in 1839. He in turn sold to a group including Henry H. Seabrook (manager), DeLafayette Schanck, and Thomas V. Arrowsmith in 1847.

In 1840, William Jacques built the Pavilion Hotel just in from the docks on the southeast corner of Broad and First Streets. In the hotel was an office for a line of stages running between Keyport and Freehold, the county seat, with several stops in between. The area was a beehive of activity. One stage owner whose stages ran to Keyport from Freehold was Elisha Thompson, who held mail contracts for the run from 1844 to 1856. The mails were carried by the stagecoaches, and then the steamboats, to New York and beyond. The first line of stages was established in 1836 to run between Keyport and Long Branch. The Keyport terminus for these was the Mansion House, an inn just up the hill from the Pavilion Hotel.

In 1847, the Keyport & Middletown Point Company bought the *Joseph E. Coffee*, a boat built by Benjamin Terry while he was still in New York. (Chapter 6 provides the story of Benjamin Terry and ship building in Keyport, but this chapter will address only those ships built for the local steamboat companies.) When the *Joseph E. Coffee* was sold to a southern company, the steamboat line ran the *John Hart*, the *Wilson Small*, and then the *Chingarora*. In 1853, Benjamin Terry, now in Keyport, built the steamboat *Keyport* for Henry Seabrook and his company. The *Keyport* was a very popular boat, and because it carried the mail, was referred to as the "mail line." It would leave Keyport in the early morning and return from New York in the mid-afternoon. Sometimes it would stop at Fort Hamilton and, early in her career, at Cliffwood Beach in deference to an incorporator of the line, Henry L. Clark.

The company had the *Matteawan* built for them in 1862 to replace the *Keyport* and she ran for 18 years. Leaving Keyport daily at 7:30 or 8:00 a.m. except Sundays, she would return from the city at 3:00 or 4:00 p.m. Usually, she would travel through the Narrows and stop at Fort Hamilton, but in bad weather she would take the inland route through the Jersey Kills and stop at Tottenville, Rossville, and Chelsea in Staten Island. Her first captain was Thomas V. Arrowsmith, then Haddock Whitlock, and later Henry E. Bishop.

The Keyport & Middletown Point Steamboat Company, which leased and later bought the Keyport Company dock, was not the only steamboat company running out of Keyport. In 1865, farmers from Holmdel and Captain Christian Emson incorporated the Farmers' Transportation Company in order to cope with large quantities of produce. They built the Holmdel Dock near the old Keyport Dock, and they placed the steamer *Holmdel* on the line. During the summer schedule, she would sometimes make two trips to New York, and even then not be able to carry all of the produce brought to the Holmdel Dock. During the winter schedule, which was usually only two or three trips a week, she would carry tons of ice and Christmas trees and other evergreens such as holly. Her captains were George W. Johnson, Henry E. Ackerson, John S. Conover, and then James G. Taylor. Built by Benjamin Terry with a depth of eight and a half feet, she was primarily a freight boat, but a few passengers were carried for a fare of 25¢. In the fall, when the freight demands diminished, she

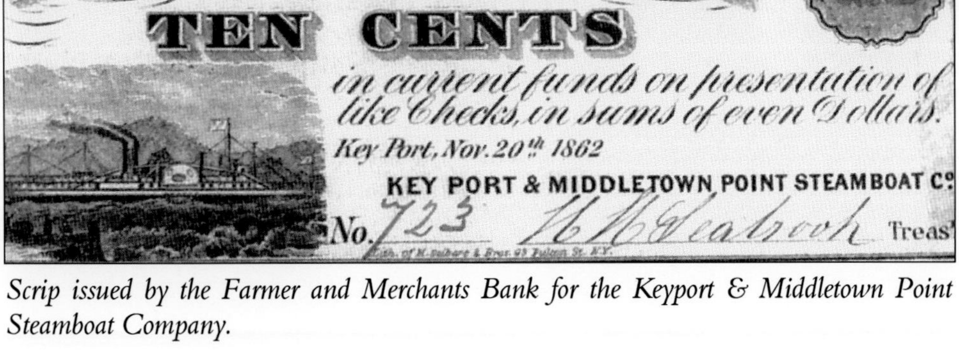

Scrip issued by the Farmer and Merchants Bank for the Keyport & Middletown Point Steamboat Company.

would take fishing parties out off the coast. The Farmers' Transportation Company lasted about ten years before being sold in March 1875 to George Schanck and De Lafayette Conover, who continued to operate the *Holmdel* at a profit.

A third company ran in competition with the Keyport & Middletown Point Steamboat Company for a short time. Edward Ellsworth, a New York merchant, acquired the Terry boat *D.R. Martin* in 1863 and ran it from a dock in the Lockport section of Keyport (probably the Chingarora Dock at the foot of Atlantic Street). Passenger rates were dropped by both companies from 25¢ to 10¢. After a few months of competition, Ellsworth conceded and withdrew from running traffic out of Keyport. Eventually, in 1865, he sold the *D.R. Martin* to his rivals, who chartered it to the Quartermaster Department. In 1886, the Holmdel and the Holmdel Dock were sold to Joseph Cornell of New York. In 1890, he formed the Keyport & New York Steamboat Company as a freight line.

The New York & Long Branch Railroad extended its tracks to Long Branch in 1875. By July of that year, there was a major drop in both freight and passenger traffic for the Keyport & Middletown Point Steamboat Company, which grew progressively worse. In December of 1875, the company's assets were offered for sale. In 1880, the dock was sold to Joseph Cornell, and the steamboat *Matteawan* was sold to a New York company.

Cornell continued to haul freight and provide passenger service. On June 22, 1900, his steamer *Magenta*, while carrying freight and about 100 passengers,

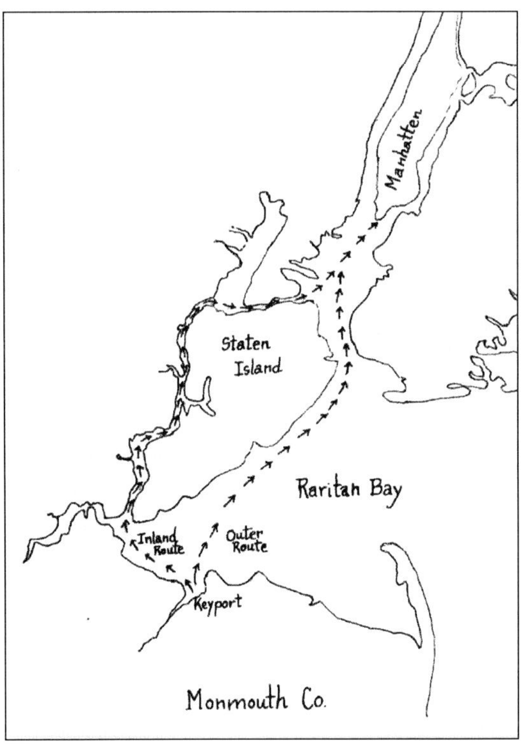

Map of inland and outer routes used for shipments to New York.

was struck by the steam lighter *Columbia*. She sustained a large hole forward of the paddle wheel but above the water line. Passengers were transferred to the *Columbia*, which was not damaged, and returned to Keyport. The freight was transferred later to the *Holmdel*, and the *Magenta* went in for repair.

On March 17, 1900, there is a brief mention of the steamer *Hudson* of the Newark and Keyport Transportation Company, stating that the *Hudson* had not sailed to Keyport yet. A week later, she arrived with a large quantity of freight. There does not appear to be any further mention of this company or steamboat.

Cornell's line continued to run a busy schedule. In August 1900, he was using the *Holmdel*, the *Magenta*, the *St. Michael*, and the *Crystal Stream*. The *Holmdel*, however, had a run of bad luck over the next year. In April 1901, she had two breakdowns involving her steering gear. In July, there were problems with government inspectors for carrying more passengers than the permit allowed. On August 6, she broke down near South Beach while on the outside run; a steam pipe broke, and she was at the mercy of the storm and dragged anchor but managed to survive.

The *Keyport Weekly* ran an editorial on May 30, 1902, complaining about the laxness of the schedules for the *Magenta* and the *Holmdel*. Many, they said, were turning to the railroads because they were more dependable. In December, however, the *Magenta* brought in an automobile for Dr. Edwin B. Reed of Asbury Park despite heavy ice in the bay. In the same month, a schooner loaded with coal for J. and J.W. Elsworth Company was stuck in the ice but managed to break through and unload at the Elsworth dock.

Also in December, the Conover lot next to the Keyport & New York dock was sold to the Staten Island Sound Transportation Company. The pilings for the Newark Transportation Company were being brought to the above site in March 1903, and the dock was completed by the middle of July.

The steamer *Magenta* was sold in March to Charles English of New York in order to settle claims against her. Cornell was able to settle all claims against the *Holmdel*, but control of the Keyport Dock was up in the air because of a mortgage held by English. The Keyport & New York Company reorganized and was able to resume freight traffic in May, yet the town found itself without any passenger service. Despite the mortgage, both the Keyport and Holmdel Docks were in use on June 19, one for incoming goods and the other for outgoing goods. A week later, it was announced that the Keyport Dock would be sold by the sheriff.

There was still a clamor for a passenger boat out of Keyport. Captain Asbury F. Walling, working for the Keyport & New York Company, convinced them to obtain a suitable boat. On July 6, the *Pokanoket* was put into service to ferry passengers. By July 17, there was a complete turnover in service as suddenly four steamboats besides the *Pokanoket*, all freighters, were put to use. The Keyport & New York Company had the *Holmdel* and the *Eagle*. The Staten Island Transportation Company had the *Wyckoff* and the *Nanticoke*. On July 15, when the *Nanticoke* arrived in Keyport, dredging was not complete for the new dock, so it pulled into the Keyport Dock and asked for water. They were refused by their

The Steamboat Holmdel. *It ran for the Farmers' Transportation Company.*

rival company, and it took a threat of turning off all water by water commissioners to provide aid for the boat.

A week later, there was an almost unbelievable scene at the waterfront. There was an endless stream of farmers' wagons converging on the corner of Broad and First Streets by the docks. Both companies had sent out canvassers throughout the countryside to urge shipping via their respective companies. In addition, both had touters along the lines of wagons proclaiming the merits of their shipping companies. These lines were about even for the Wallabout Market in Brooklyn between the *Nanticoke* and the *Eagle*. Earlier, the *Holmdel* had carried off most of the traffic for the New York market, but the *Wyckoff* had received about 400 packages. Unfortunately, 1903 was a poor season for farmers because of adverse weather, so the amount of business did not merit so many steamboats. In addition, the *Nanticoke* was of deep draft and experienced delays because of tides, which brought her to market late. As a result, the company withdrew her from the route.

On July 27, the sheriff sold the Keyport Dock for $150 subject to all prior encumbrances. The unknown buyers were represented by Mayor Ogden. Prior encumbrances included a mortgage of $10,000. When this remained unpaid, foreclosure proceedings were brought in August.

The *Pokanoket* had some engine problems on one trip, but continued to provide passenger service. There were indications, however, of people not supporting this service enough to make it a paying proposition. In September, the owners of the *Eagle* withdrew her from the Keyport/New York route, which cut back on the freight boats serving the town. In October, the company placed the *Pokanoket* on the Wallabout freight run.

The Staten Island Transportation Company had become the New York & New Jersey Steamboat Company by March 1904. That same month, they bought out all assets of the Keyport & New York Company. The latter had lost money on running the passenger service with the *Pokanoket*, and even the freight service with the *Holmdel* had not been profitable because of the poor season for farmers. The new company planned to abandon the Holmdel Dock and improve the Keyport Dock, but there were no plans to provide passenger service. The company secured the *William V. Wilson* for the Keyport run.

The Keyport Board of Trade threatened in April 1904 to cut off freight for the company if it did not provide passenger service. They put on a very slow boat, the *St. Michael*, which took the longer inside route and carried 25 passengers. The trip took so long that the passengers left the boat at Perth Amboy or Tottenville.

The *Keyport Weekly* ran several editorials, and people started talking about forming a new company to provide customer service. In March 1905, the Board of Trade recommended to the town commissioners that Keyport build a steamboat dock for a passenger steamer to come in to. The commissioners contended that the town charter did not allow for such construction, only for streets, erecting waterworks, buying horses, etc. Druggist R.O. Walling suggested tongue-in-cheek to build a dock and put a barn for the town horses on it. It was pointed out that the borough of South Amboy built a dock, so a committee was formed to see what could be done. They found a boat suitable for passenger service, the *Adelaide*. J.A. Johnson of Sea Bright was willing to operate it but could not obtain docking privileges in Keyport. On June 30, 1906, it was sold for use in the Boston area.

In April 1907, Mr. Ward, superintendent of the New York & New Jersey Transportation Company, requested permission to erect a fence along the company's property across the end of Broad Street. The Board of Town Commissioners took no action on the request but noted that this would cut off what had been considered public thoroughfare and access to the bay.

In May 1908, the prospects were very bright for obtaining passenger steamboat service for Keyport. A suitable boat had been found that had not even been in commission yet, the *Happy Day*, at a cost of only $60,000. A group of local people went to Shooters Island to see her in J.G. Schanck's launch. The best plan to purchase the boat and start service seemed to be to organize a company with a capital of $75,000 and issue stock at $10 per share. A meeting was called at the armory for May 14, 1907, and there was great enthusiasm that the plan would come to fruition. By the end of June, a closer evaluation of the *Happy Day* found it requiring an additional expenditure of $25,000 on the boat before federal inspectors would permit a license to be issued.

In January 1908, Dr. Bogardus sold to the New York & New Jersey Transportation Company waterfront property just to the west of the company's docks. In 1909, The Starin Company of New York looked at the feasibility of running a service from Keyport. In the meantime, a dock was built and passenger steamboat service started from Keansburg. Elsewhere on the Keyport waterfront, 400,000 feet of lumber was off-loaded from a schooner and delivered to the Chingarora Dock at Atlantic Street.

In 1910, the Keansburg Steamboat Company purchased the *Nantasket* for their service to New York and renamed it the *Keansburg*. In April, President Hopkins of the New York & New Jersey Transportation Company offered to charter a boat and provide passenger service to New York. Freight on the boat would not be considered, and the borough of Keyport would have to guarantee to make up any deficit. A meeting of Keyport businessmen was held on May 6, but attendance was poor and no conclusions could be reached. The summer of 1910 was a bad one for farmers, and the freight service suffered accordingly.

Finally in 1911, seven years after the first talk of building a dock for the purpose, one was built and passenger service started. In May, P.A. Nickerson of the Hudson Navigation Company, owner of the *Christina*, offered to provide steamboat service for Keyport if docking could be provided. Meetings were held and, after discussion of various sites, the decision was reached to build a dock from a strip of land offered by the owner of the Pavilion Hotel just east of the New York & New Jersey docks. A company was formed to take over the charter of the Keyport Company. Mr. Hopkins of the New York & New Jersey Company offered to lease the Holmdel Dock for $1 per year for 5 years if the new Keyport Company would agree to hold service to only passengers. His offer was rejected. Pilings were purchased from Matawan and a contract was let for dock construction at the end of June. It was completed by August 11 and service started a week later. In September the New York & New Jersey people started to build a fence blocking off the end of Broad Street; the Keyport people tore it down. The contract for boat service went to George C. Weidenmayer of Newark instead of P.A. Nickerson. The *Majestic* was the first boat to run on the new route. By October, it became evident that there were enough passengers but not enough freight to make the service pay. In November, the New York & New Jersey Company brought suit against the Keyport Company.

In May 1911, the Keansburg Company announced that automobile buses would be provided to take passengers between the trolley and the steamboat. There was a very successful excursion to take passengers from Keyport to see the warships in the North River during the summer. When the Christmas season arrived, the *Majestic* hauled great loads of greens to the New York market. There was one incident of the *Majestic* getting stuck in the mud at the Keyport dock and another on a sand bar off East Point in the fog. Special trolley accommodations were provided for the delayed travelers.

1912 opened with a Keyport Company banquet given for George C. Weidenmayer, who operated the *Majestic* on the line. It is also noted that the repair and overhaul of the steamboat was complete and service would resume in March. In June, about 900 excursionists arrived at Keyport on the *Minerva*, landing at the new dock. The New York & New Jersey Company won the lawsuit over the fence with a verdict of 6¢ and costs; In July, they erected a new fence. In August, the Keansburg Steamboat Company started running their boats for passenger service between Keyport and New York as well as between Keansburg and New York using the *Keansburg* and the *Chrystenah*. In September, the *Chrystenah* was

Behind the Boat Club dock is the Chingarora dock loaded with lumber.

withdrawn, and the Keansburg Company ordered a new boat to be named the *New Point Comfort*. There were complaints about the service, particularly about an October Sunday trip when the boat returned from New York—with 75 Keyport passengers aboard—docked at Keansburg, and refused to run on to Keyport. On December 25, the *Keansburg* was put into drydock to resume service on April 1.

The Keyport Company held its annual meeting at Keough's Hall on January 15, 1913. In May, they persuaded the Keansburg Company to put on a daily freight boat. In July, the *Keyport*, while moored at the Gansevoort Street pier in New York, was struck by a tug and disabled. The *Huntington* was designated to take her place.

Occasionally crimes were committed on the steamboats and docks. A knife fight ensued on board the *Sagamore* while docked at the foot of Broad Street in August 1913. Edward Jenkins was treated by a physician and his assailant taken into custody. A month later, D.H. Weeks, a former deckhand of the Keansburg Company, was beaten badly by mates of the steamer *Keyport* for talking about unions. Also in September, Angelo Cantaloupo was arrested and charged with stealing produce barrels from the New York & New Jersey docks. In September 1916, there was a shooting on the New York & New Jersey Company docks. Every Saturday, after the deck hands were paid off, there would be a craps game on the docks. On September 16, "Peachie" Jackson was holding the stakes, when George Cooper went for Benjamin Turner with a knife; Turner pulled out a gun and shot Cooper four times. "Peachie" seized the gun and held Turner for the authorities.

In November 1913, the Keansburg Company drove pilings and dredged out a basin to arrange for wintering all of its boats in Keyport. In July 1914, the Keyport

Company sold its dock to the Keansburg Steamboat Company for $8,000. It had debts of $7,200, which were paid, and distribution of the balance was made to stockholders. Thus ended Keyport's venture into providing passenger service on steamboats. The Keansburg Company ran a boat from Keyport to Keansburg to connect with the New York boats during the summer of 1920 and talked about running a regular service to New York from Keyport in 1921, but no further traffic ensued. The area east of the dock was dredged, and for many years the company stored the *Pocahontas*, the *Mobjack*, the *Smithfield*, the *City of New York*, and the *City of Keansburg* at the docks. Some were run during the summers, and some just remained docked in Keyport. Severe storms that hit the town took their toll on both boats and docks. The unnamed hurricane of November 1950 destroyed all that remained except the *City of Keansburg*, and it sailed out of Keyport not long after.

The New York & New Jersey Steamboat Company continued to haul freight to and from Keyport. In April 1922, the *Fannie*, one of the company's boats, lay on the mud flats off shore with a leak; repairs were made. Boats run by the company were the *S.S. Wyckoff*, the *Holmdel Sagamore*, the *St. Michaels*, the *Fannie*, the *Industry*, and the *Kill Van Kull*. The *Kill Van Kull* was the last boat to haul freight for the company. Thus ended the steamboat days in Keyport. They were a vibrant and vital link in the transportation chain for Monmouth County, and the longest and greatest use of them was from the little town of Keyport.

Freight boats of the New York & New Jersey Steamboat company at the Keyport dock.

5. Center of Commerce and Industry

With Keyport already the major port for northern Monmouth County, it was only natural that there would be a buildup of business in the new village. As you will find from reading the next chapter, ship building on a major scale started almost immediately.

As a major port, there was a need for hotels. In 1837, the Keyport Company built the Atlantic Hotel to provide lodging for incoming passengers. It was located on the south side of West Front Street, a few doors west of Broad Street. When it was destroyed by fire in 1877, it was not rebuilt. In 1840, William Jacques built the Pavilion Hotel on the southeast corner of Broad and First Streets; it burned in 1851 and was rebuilt by D.L.F. Schenck. It was constructed on high ground with wide porches overlooking the bay, lawns gently sloping to First Street, and its own wide and shaded beach across the road. It had 70 guest rooms, a gracious dining room, wide porches, and access to the docks next to its beaches. A third major hotel was erected shortly after the Pavilion; the Mansion House was built by George Dickinson (Ellis has it as Davison) on the northeast corner of Broad and East Front Streets next to the Pavilion. Like the Atlantic, it was completely destroyed by fire in 1877, but the Mansion House was rebuilt (this time as a brick structure) by John S. Sproul shortly after the fire. Other smaller hotels were built, such as the Bayside Hotel and the Washington Hotel. When the trolleys came, Jersey Central Traction Company would build its offices and waiting room on First Street next to the lawns and flower gardens of the Pavilion Hotel.

On March 12, 1833, when the town was only three years old, a post office was opened in Keyport. The first postmaster was Leonard Walling, and the office was in the store of Captain Joseph D. Hoff.

The earliest newspapers changed owners and also names over the period from 1845 to 1855. The *Union* became The *Olive Branch*, which through political leanings became the *Democratic Banner*, then following a change of ownership became The *N.J. Standard*. The papers of that era were weekly and consisted of four pages. Of the four pages, two were almost entirely advertising.

A thread running through these papers, with regard to Keyport, was references to the Kearney suit or the Kearney case. By 1854, the case was in the United States Supreme Court. The Kearney orphans objected to having the Kearney plantation whisked out from under them while they were defenseless children, and they were trying to retrieve what they considered their birthright. In the years from 1829, when the Orphans' Court sale had taken the plantation from them, to 1854 when the case was in the Supreme Court for decision, a great deal of change had taken place.

A review of the advertising in the above-cited papers provides an interesting outline of change to Keyport. By 1847, there were two significant hotels with advertisements: the Keyport Pavilion and the Atlantic Hotel. The steamer *Joseph E. Coffee* with Captain J.T. Weeks was serving the village. Robert M. Selleck had a saddle and harness manufactory, and B. Evesson had a bakery with an interesting assortment of items.

By 1852, the Keyport & Middletown Point Steamboat Company incorporated, and the company was running the steamer *Wilson Small* under Captain H. Whitlock from both Keyport and Middletown Point. Rufus Ogden was now in the harness and saddle business. A boarding and day school had been established at Van Doren Hall. Stout, Patterson & Company were selling boots, shoes, and clothing opposite the post office. Wilson Brown was selling dry goods, hats, caps, and shoes. Finally, there was an obituary for Dr. George T. Taylor, who had been practicing medicine for several years in Keyport. (The first physician, however, was Dr. John Griggs who opened his office in 1833.)

In 1853, there was an expansion of the medical profession in Keyport. Dr. J. Edgar Arrowsmith took over the practice of Dr. Taylor, Dr. W.C. Lewis had an office next door to P.P. Conover's store, Dr. E.W. Owen had an office at Judge

Lufburrow & Walling Carriage factory, located in the Mechanicsville section of Keyport.

Clark's drug store, and Dr. E. Ensell Price was at J.S. Forman's in Lockport. Dr. Price, incidentally, took over the practice of Dr. Edwin Ensell.

In 1853, the steamer *Wilson Small* had been replaced by the *John Hart* with the same Captain H. Whitlock. The *N.J. Standard* office was at Lloyd's Drug Store (another drug store). Cuttrell's Paint and Oil Store was in Brown's Point presumably near the Cuttrell Ship Yard. The March 23, 1853, issue mentioned the launch of a 50-ton schooner from his yard for use in the Shrewsbury River trade. Gilbert S. Dye had established a tin and wooden ware store opposite Wilson Brown's. Rufus Ogden was still in the harness and saddle business and Stout, Patterson & Company in the clothing business. J. Rightmire was starting to advertise his tailor shop, which was established in 1851.

Thomas Carhart had started a Carriage Manufactory in the southern end of town in 1844 and had sold it to Samuel and Timothy Carhart in 1850. In 1853, they advertised as built-to-order: close carriages, rockaways, two-seat carriages, buggies, trotting wagons, sulkies, and any kind of farm wagon. They had in their employ from 30 to 40 mechanics. The operation was so big and so well known that to this day the area of Keyport south of Highway 36 is referred to as Mechanicsville. Maps & Shaw opened a general store in this section in 1853. Prior to the advent of the carriage works, there was only one house in this section of Keyport.

In 1854, most of the businesses mentioned above were still in full swing. Three more clothing stores opened: Samuel Winterton, E. Stout & Son, and J. Abeel deForeest. Warner & Walling opened a Lumber, Coal & Hardware business. There were two steamers leaving daily for New York: the *Keyport* with Captain T.V. Arrowsmith and the *John Hart* with Captain H. Whitlock. There is also reference to the steamer *Keyport* lying at Union City (which encompasses what today is Union Beach).

In 1860, the Carhart carriage works was sold to John Herbert, who leased it to Theodore W. Aumack, who in turn continued the business until 1896. It then became Lufburrow & Walling until Mr. Lufburrow retired in 1904. During the entire history of the factory (1844–1914) all types of carriages were made and repaired, horses were shod, and toward the end of its long history the company made alterations to truck and auto bodies.

Bedle's lumber mill opened in 1854 on Necus Pond and East Front Street. Necus Pond extended from the present-day "bottom of the hill" of East Front Street to the lawns of the T.V. Arrowsmith mansion (the present-day Masonic Lodge). James Bedle also built a stately brick home at 80 Main Street in the same year. Two years later, Andrew McDowell built the first gristmill in Keyport. Stephen G. Lambertson bought the mill in 1865 and operated it for several years.

By 1851, there were three brick manufacturers in the 60-acre tract at the eastern end of Keyport: William Garrison, Kickerson & Kimburk, and Ackerman & Blauvelt. By 1889, all three had been replaced by Thomas H. Robbins. Bricks from these companies went into many of the brick homes built in the 1850s and into the brick commercial buildings along Front and Broad Streets after the fire of 1877. By 1901, when Jersey Central Traction Company was building the powerhouse and car barns, bricks were brought in from the Cliffwood area.

Banks are an important element in the success of any town. The People's Bank tried in 1836, 1854, 1858, 1859, and 1862 to operate in Keyport, but each time it failed. The first successful banking operation was the First National Bank of Keyport in 1884 with a starting capital of $50,000. The first president was Michael Taylor and the first cashier Garret S. Jones. The bank was reorganized in 1889 as the Keyport Banking Company, changing from the national system of banks to the state system. The original building was just east of the current building on the corner of Broad and East Front Streets. When the McKinney Drug Store building on the corner was razed in 1928, the current bank building was constructed. There have been many mergers over the years, but under different names the Keyport Banking Company has continued at the same site to the present day.

In 1889, it was felt that there was room for another bank in town. The Peoples' National Bank was established with Thomas Burrowes as its first president and William H. Tuthill as cashier. Their original capital stock was also $50,000. The introductory building was just south of the southwest corner of Broad and Front Streets. When they constructed a new building in the middle of the block on the north side of West Front Street, their old building was sold to the Keyport Hebrew Congregation as a synagogue. The Peoples' National Bank has also seen many mergers and changes of name, but continues to serve Keyport from the West Front Street location to this day.

In 1861, 17-year-old Adam Salz came to America, landing in New York. On June 21, 1864, he came to Keyport and opened a dry goods store. The fire of 1877 burned his business to the ground. But he had established himself so well with the people of Keyport that the owners of the Walling estate erected a building for him on the southwest corner of Broad and Front Streets where he continued his business. Over the years, he expanded the size of his store to include the adjacent building. The store also expanded to become a department store, which occupied three floors and a basement with an area of 30,000 square feet. Around 1910, he remodeled the entire front of the two buildings to provide five large show windows and installed an elaborate electric lighting system.

In addition to serving Keyport and the surrounding area, A. Salz & Company shipped to Philadelphia, Salt Lake City, and San Francisco. There were many anniversary sales over the years; its fiftieth in 1914 saw crowds in the thousands, and the occasion was enhanced with music from several bands. In 1918, there was a fire that started in the clothing department and threatened the entire store, but quick work by the fire department minimized damage. In 1920, the partnership of A. and Henry Salz, Inc. offered a bonus/profit-sharing plan to its employees. At that point, there were also stores in Red Bank and Springfield, Massachusetts, and stores planned in Hartford and New Haven, Connecticut. In 1925, the Salzes retired and sold off all assets.

In addition to A. Salz & Company, there were other clothing stores. W.S. Wallace was the successor to T.L. Seabrook's Clothing in 1906; continuing in business until the 1990s. Conklin's Men & Boys Shop started in 1928 and also continued until the last decade of the twentieth century.

William H. Cherry and Francis W. Tilton started their careers working for Theodore Aumack at his carriage works in the Mechanicsville section. In 1875, they formed the partnership of Tilton & Cherry to make carriages on Elizabeth Street near Main Street. Their business grew so fast that in 1885 they bought property on the southwest corner of Broad and Mott (now Maple) Streets, moved their shop to the new location, and enlarged it. In addition to carriages and wagons, they produced bay tools (clam rakes, oyster tongs, etc.). In May 1909, they built another stagecoach for Edward A. Smalley for the Rocky Hill–Princeton run and another stagecoach for I.B. Thompson of Lakewood. In September of that year Phelps Cherry, Charles Russell, William H. Cherry, and George Smith incorporated as the Commercial Car Company. The intention of the company was to produce automobiles for commercial use following the patents of Mr. Russell. Production of the body and finishing was the responsibility of the Cherrys and all machine work was the responsibility of Mr. Twist of Philadelphia. By October, they were ready for production. This author could find no further mention of the Commercial Car Company, and it appears that these plans went nowhere. Tilton & Cherry did build a body for Raritan Hose Company in 1917. In April 1918, Francis W. Tilton and William H. Cherry sold their carriage factory property and retired.

In 1865, T.S.R. Brown and Richard B. Walling opened a lumber and coal business on the west side of Atlantic Street between First Street and Second

People's National Bank at its original location. It was later the temple for the Keyport Hebrew Congregation and is now an art studio.

Street. Mr. Walling died in 1871 and Mr. Brown bought his interests; Mr. Brown's son Thomas joined the firm but died in 1879. The business continued as T.S.R. Brown Company until Mr. Brown died in 1892. It continued as T.S.R. Brown Estate Company until it was bought by George H. Conover in 1916. The company had the Chingarora Dock at the foot of Atlantic Street from about 1865 until the early part of the twentieth century. The coal business was abandoned in 1910 to concentrate on the lumber business. Lumber was shipped in from many places along the Atlantic coast to the Chingarora Dock. While operating as T.S.R. Brown Estate Company in 1910, manager R.R. Brown had a sawmill erected on Mott (now Maple) Street near the lumber storage yard.

George H. Conover and Charles I. Young had started a sash, blind, and millwork company near the armory on First Street before 1900. In 1901, Conover & Young built a planing mill just south of the railroad on Division Street. The planers, band and rip saws, and other machinery were on the ground floor as well as an office. The upstairs was used for storage. When George H. Conover bought Charles I. Young's interests in 1912, the firm became Conover Lumber Company and continued under that name until the firm's dissolution in 1982. The above mentioned purchase of T.S.R. Brown Estate in 1916 made Conover Lumber the largest lumber company in the area.

Tilton & Cherry after the move to the southwest corner of Broad Street and Maple Place.

Robert West started in business as a rag carpet weaver in a small store on Front Street in 1859. Gradually he increased the scope of his business to include selling not only carpets, but rugs and furniture as well. He moved to larger quarters a few years later, and then in 1873 he built a large store on the corner of First and Church Streets. In the beginning, the sign in front of the business simply read R. West and then R. West Company. Harry West bought his father's interest in the business in 1914 and later changed the name to West Furniture Company. In 1923, the store on the corner of First and Church was enlarged with showrooms and warehouse facilities to total 45,000 square feet. A canopy was built around the street edges over the sidewalks. An earlier advertisement in 1916 urged the purchase of Hoosier Kitchen Cabinets at $1 down and $1 per week, as "$1.00 puts the cabinet in your home for Xmas." Over the years, West Furniture established a reputation of selling the very finest furniture at modest prices. When the main store burned to the ground in an intense conflagration in 1976, the company moved its operations to two older buildings on the corner of East Front and Church Streets and annexed the old post office building on the corner of East Front and Osborn Streets. The company went out of business in1996.

John G. Schanck was in the coal and ice business in 1889 and sold the business to Jesse N. Beers in 1908. Ice was cut from ponds in those days and stored in heavily-insulated ice houses. In May 1909, Louis Stultz Jr. and his brother-in-law Russell Clark built the Hygeia Ice Plant on Division Street just south of the railroad tracks. The plant had a 70-foot iron stack and 4-inch water mains running into it. At the time, the plant had a capacity of 25 tons of ice per day, and by 1926 it had a 75-ton per day capacity. In the fall of 1911, the company started dealing in coal on a small scale, buying it in 1-ton lots at the docks. In 1916, as Louis Stultz Jr. Fuel Company, the business established a yard on Broad Street just south of the tracks. Coal deliveries increased to as much as 55 tons per day. In 1921, the company added the feed business and installed a flourmill. In 1923, it was converted to a feed mill handling all feeds. The oil business started in the 1930s. The first deliveries were made using 5-gallon cans until the first oil truck was purchased. There were other fuel companies in Keyport in competition with Stultz. J. & J.W. Elsworth were early coal dealers. Judson Hopla had a yard on Third Street. Schanck, Inc. was across from the high school on Broad Street, and Hollywood Oil was at Six Corners near St. Joseph's Catholic Church. The only fuel company in Keyport today is Stultz Fuel Company.

McKinney's Drug Store, on the southeast corner of Broad and Front Streets, was for many years the largest in Keyport. Rufus O. Walling worked for pharmacist Alfred W. Hoff after graduating from Keyport High School and graduated from the New York College of Pharmacy in 1897. He purchased McKinney's from the A.W. Hoff estate in 1898 and ran his pharmacy there until 1926. In 1901, he opened a branch in Matawan and later sold it to Sanford.

William E. Warn learned the drug business in 1868 with Dr. Hodgson. After serving his apprenticeship, he opened his own drug store on First Street near

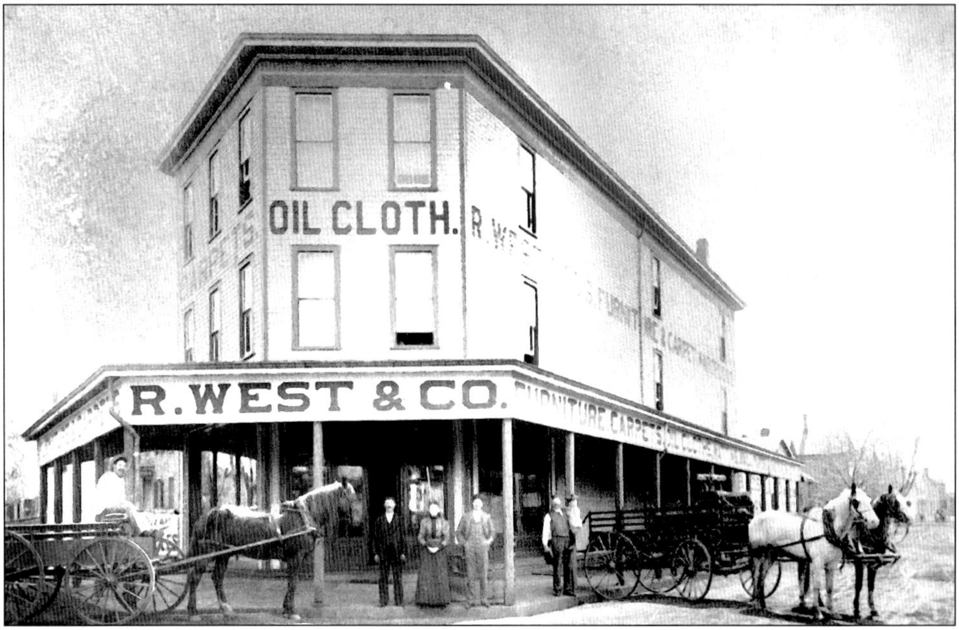

West Furniture Company was on the corner of First and Church Streets for many years.

Church Street. In 1878, he bought the lot next door and erected a new store at 55 First Street with living quarters behind facing the bay. The business prospered, and Mr. Warn took an active part in Keyport affairs as commissioner, mayor, fireman, and president of the People's National Bank. In 1911, he installed a new "iceless" soda fountain in his store. He sold the pharmacy to Macy Carhart in 1915. Henry Hopkins, who had clerked in the store, entered the New York College of Pharmacy in 1904 and continued to work part time.

In April 1920, Dr. Henry Hopkins purchased the drug business from Macy Carhart; the business retained the name Warn's Drug Store. Dr. Hopkins had enlisted as a private in the Medical Corps during World War I, became an instructor in Materia Medica Pharmacy and Chemistry at the NCO School, then became a sergeant, and as sergeant first-class was assigned to the Chemical Warfare Service. After being discharged in September 1919, he resumed his duties at Warn's Drug Store until his purchase of the store. Mr. Carhart continued as a pharmacist at the store. The business continued to prosper and Dr. Hopkins opened another pharmacy at 42 Carr Avenue in Keansburg.

In 1924, Morrissey & Walker Builders erected a modern store for a pharmacy at 27 Front Street next to the People's National Bank, and Dr. Hopkins opened another store there as a partner to Morrissey & Walker. In July 1930, he bought out the Morrissey & Walker interests in Hopkins Drug Stores, Inc., with Morrissey & Walker retaining a mortgage. Following the market crash in 1929 and during the Depression that followed, Dr. Hopkins lost the Front Street store in a foreclosure along with all furnishings and drug supplies. He also had to close the Keansburg store, but continued at the First Street location until his death in January 1972.

Cigar manufacturing was a Keyport industry for many years. The Boyd's Directory of 1889–1890 lists as cigar manufacturers: George W. Waitt, Hugh J. McCabe (Front Street), S.P. Dey & Company (First Street), Edward Howard (Front Street), and M. & I. Naftal (Front Street). In June 1908, the Keyport Cigar Factory opened for business on Front Street. In October 1913, H.H. Winters, the local cigar manufacturer, opened a cigar and tobacco store in the Melvin Yard building.

Perhaps the oldest soda bottling company in Keyport was that of Abram Morris Jr. in the mid 1880s; he sold to his brother Elmer in 1892. Lemon fizz and orange were popular flavors. His shop on the northeast corner of Third and Division Streets was small with only a bottling machine, a facility for cleaning bottles, and a storage area. For Morris and his later competitors, all bottles had the bottler's name and a warning that the bottles were not to be sold or discarded embossed in the glass. E.E. Morris sold to H.J. Cohen and his sons Maurice and Edward as Keyport Bottling Works. They built a hollow tile building on Division Street in the mid–1920s and moved the operation there. They delivered shipments by horse and wagon to the steamboat docks for shipment to New York. Maurice Cohen left the business in 1923. In 1933, Edward Cohen and his younger brother Harry went into the liquor business and moved the soda business to the basement of the liquor store in 1938. Harry P. Disbrow had a soda bottling business from 1887 to about 1950 in the Browns Point section of Keyport. Other bottlers were Herman O. Bauer, Joseph Mauer, William Mauer, and Edwin H. Pelton.

In 1923, J. Schuttenberg opened a delicatessen at 31 West Front Street. Prior to opening the store, he worked in New York and would buy rounds of cheese and sleeves of lunchmeats and sell them by the pound from his home. He provided such quality and variety that he created great demand. In the store, he provided a vast array of foods. On a Friday or Saturday, his customers were packed solidly into the store and the whole Shuttenberg family and others worked diligently for hours on end, particularly on Fridays and Saturdays. When Mr. Shuttenberg retired, he sold the business in the 1950s to "Buster" Brown, who continued the business for a few more years.

D.E. Mahoney came to Keyport in 1880 and opened a grocery store at 41–43 First Street. He soon added a flour, feed, and hay business. When it prospered, he opened stores in other towns. By 1911, he had seven more stores in South Amboy, Freehold, Matawan, Port Monmouth, Marlboro, and two in Keansburg. His home was just east of Warn's Drug Store on the bay, and he had a 118-acre farm to grow most of the fresh fruits and vegetables he sold, as well as the hay. In 1906, he employed his niece Anna May Mahoney as a stenographer and bookkeeper. In 1907, he bought the old carriage factory on Main Street, Matawan, and moved his grocery into it. In November 1907, he bought a Rapid brand delivery automobile at the auto show at Grand Central Palace. By 1912, he had a second building in Keyport on Front Street. Louis Costa, who would later open a luncheonette, soda fountain, and tobacco store on Front Street, worked for D.E. Mahoney in 1912.

His store on First Street had a corrugated metal awning over the sidewalk, and every morning a large array of produce would be hauled out for display under the canopy. The Great Depression took its toll on Mahoney; he lost all of his other stores, then his home, and died quietly at an advanced age all alone in the quarters above his store in 1942.

In December 1896, the Keyport Improvement Company, a non-profit organization for promoting business in Keyport, offered a building it had erected to the Unterberg shirt factory on condition that Unterberg continue in business there until at least 1900. The company agreed, opened for business, and employed about 80 local people there. However, in November 1902, the factory burned to the ground. It was reopened in May 1903 in the same building as the Cutlery factory.

In May 1901, Benjamin B. Ogden, a local lawyer, was elected mayor of the town of Keyport to succeed John G. Schanck. On December 5, Secretary Benjamin B. Ogden presented his annual report of the status of the Second Keyport Loan Association. It had had a very good year—funds belonging to the organization had gone from $163,427 to $182,037. The following year he reported that the association had earned 7.7 percent. In February 1903, Benjamin B. Ogden was re-appointed postmaster in Keyport. In May, he was re-elected mayor and served on the finance committee. On September 12, 1903, he left town, leaving his wife and family behind amidst rumors of financial difficulties and the disappearance of several trust funds of which he had been in charge. He sold his horses and carriages to William Van Brunt just prior to his departure. A review of real estate transfers showed a massive number of them by Benjamin Ogden within a short time before his departure. Coincidentally, a loss was discovered from the safe at the post office. He was removed as postmaster in October. Judge J. Franklin Fort called the grand jury and charged them with reference to the defalcations and use of trust funds by counsellor Benjamin B. Ogden. An examination of the books found a deficiency in the loan association of $5,289. The Ogden creditors met on November 2 to act on bankruptcy procedures. At a meeting of creditors on November 17, Sheriff Bogardus was selected as trustee; those present represented claims of about $33,000. By 1905, the indebtedness was estimated between $100,000 and $200,000, a reward of $250 had been offered for him, and a man had been arrested in Tennessee who matched his description. The person arrested turned out to be an innocent party and Benjamin B. Ogden was never found.

One of the casualties of the Ogden disappearance, however, was the American Cutlery Company; Ogden was the treasurer. In November 1903, the company went into receivership. The Unterberg shirt factory in the same building had to close as well. Cornelius Ackerson, the receiver appointed, requested permission to re-open to fill outstanding orders and accumulate some capital to satisfy creditors and he received permission. The company, however, was beset by other difficulties. In February 1904, the authorities arrested George C. Hatch and charged him with embezzling $15,000 from the company. In October 1906, the business was sold to the Sherman Razor Company. The Keyport Board of Trade had met and subscribed $1,500 in capital to move the Sherman Razor Company

Interior of Warn's Drug Store. Shown left to right are Cliff Morrell, Henry Hopkins, Macy Carhart (owned the store during World War I), William E. Warn (original owner). Picture courtesy Stockton Hopkins.

to the new site. The new company moved in and by January 1907 was a beehive of activity, producing knives and razors.

As suddenly as the Sherman Razor Company had started in Keyport it also ended. In July 1907, it was in the hands of receivers. In April, the company had advertised for capital. A group purportedly representing an owner of coal reserves worth $10 million took Sherman Razor Company notes worth $150,000 discounted at 6 percent and in return promised a large loan with the initial payment in cash due by the company's next payroll. Instead, the company received a worthless draft and found that their notes were being peddled by people with no financial standing. The culprits were arrested, but the company went under.

The Davis Radio Company was incorporated in October 1922 and opened its doors at 27 East Front Street in Keyport. J. Burgess Davis had several patents pending on various radio devices. One of these was exhibited at the radio show at Grand Central Palace in New York in December 1922. It was similar to the super heterodyne radio and on the cutting edge. Another Keyport resident, Frank Carnahan, independently invented a new sounding board for radios. He connected a Radiola radio through an eliminator to a sounding board of a piano. The result was a high fidelity sound beyond imagination for 1928.

There were many other industries as well as several commercial establishments. The Eagle Tile Works was a small operation bought by Karl Mathiesen in 1906 and enlarged. Clay was brought in from England, Florida, Tennessee, and from nearby South River. Under Mathiesen, the name changed to Keyport Tile Company. In 1912, it went to A.W. Christiani and was renamed the Architectural Tile Company. In 1909, Whiteall Tatum built a factory on Perry Street and manufactured rubber products. Later, Armstrong Cork Company moved into the Whiteall Tatum plant. In 1911, A.M. Jacoby & Company built a plant in Lockport between Second and Third Streets and moved its industrial sewing machine factory there. Early hardware stores were Force & Wyckoff, Hendrickson & Bronner, and John W. Keough. These were succeeded by the large establishment of John G. Schanck in 1911. The Keyport Hardware Company was purchased by the Gales in 1938 and became Gales Hardware Company, which has specialized in industrial supply and continues to this day.

The story of commerce and industry in Keyport parallels that of cities and towns throughout the country, however. Most commercial establishments either moved out to the highways or went out of business. Except for a few small plants, Keyport's industries have closed and it has developed into a small residential town within the New York megalopolis.

D.E. Mahoney's grocery store on the south side of First Street between Church and Broad Streets.

6. Ship Building on Shoal Waters and the Civil War

One year after Keyport was established, in 1831, John Cuttrell moved his shipbuilding operation from Compton's Creek to the new town. He operated his yard near the mouth of Matawan Creek in the Brown's Point section. While he was still at Compton's Creek, he had gained the reputation for building the finest of sloops. The tip of Brown's Point became a very busy place, with two to five large vessels under construction at any one time. There was a great demand for sailing ships to carry the volume of produce from the interior of Monmouth County to New York. There were many other customers and uses as well. One, for example, was the *E.T. Blodgett*, which was built for the slave trade. It was a two-masted schooner with a great overhanging stern, and the rudder in front of the cabin and 60 feet from the taffrail—a very unusual construction. The Cuttrell yards continued to build sailing ships for decades, but never made the transition to steamships.

The population of Keyport was less than 200 when the first of many steamships was built there in 1841. National Archives credits Richard Jacques with building the steamship *Rainbow* at the Rosevelt and Hoff yards, which were located on the Warn shore lots opposite the end of the present day Church Street.

The *Rainbow* was built for Robert L. Stevens, who had assisted in the design and construction of the *Phoenix* in 1808—one year after Robert Fulton had successfully demonstrated the use of steam power for boats with the *Clermont*. Stevens had the *Rainbow* built in Keyport and for speed, with a beam of less than 17 feet and a length of 220 feet. However, the speed was still not enough and the carrying capacity was insufficient to compete in a rapidly emerging field, so the *Rainbow* was never a money maker.

When Benjamin C. Terry arrived in Keyport around 1849, shipbuilding began in earnest. Terry had built the *Joseph E. Coffee* in New York in 1846 and it had been purchased by a Keyport and Middletown Point company headed up by Henry H. Seabrook, DeLafayette Schenck, and Thomas Arrowsmith. They were so pleased with the *Coffee's* performance that they ordered a number of other vessels from Terry. His choice of Keyport as his shipbuilding site was no doubt influenced by that order.

The first Terry shipyard was at the mouth of Luppatatong Creek, essentially where Ye Cottage Inn and Firemen's Park are today. In 1852, the first steamship laid out in the yards was the *Enoch Dean*, a side-wheeler of 194 tons and 135 feet long. Before the *Dean* was completed, the *Junior*, of 204 tons and 136 feet long, was built in five weeks and launched in June 1852. At this yard, Terry launched 16 ships of various tonnages between 1852 and 1856.

He moved his operations at about this time to a large tract of land at the foot of Myrtle Street, where he also made his residence. He received permission and installed marine railways to launch his vessels. He had been producing two to four ships per year at the first shipyard and produced only one in the transition year of 1857. At the new yard, by the Civil War years of 1862–1864 he was launching six to eight ships per year. The size of the ships varied considerably. Terry's smallest steamboat was the *Kate*, which was 86 feet long and weighed in at 56 tons; this was launched in 1853. In 1866, Terry launched the *Seawanaka*, which was 200 feet long and weighed in at 611 tons. As we can see, the Terry shipyards (in both locations) were massive operations in a very small town. Keyport in these years had a population of only a few thousand.

Four vessels were delivered to the Keyport & Middletown Point Steamboat Company: the *Keyport* in 1853, the *Thomas P. Way* in 1859, the *Thomas V. Arrowsmith* in 1861, and the *Matteawan* in 1862. The *D.R. Martin* was built for the Keyport & Middletown Point Steamboat Company, but because of dissension within the business Edward Ellsworth became the first owner and set up a steamship line from a Lockport dock in competition with the company. The last of the steamships built for Keyport service was the *Holmdel*, which was built for the Farmers Transportation Company in 1866. The *Holmdel* was not a paddle wheel ship; it was a steam propeller-driven ship, which was unusual for those days. Fourteen other Terry ships were built for passenger and freight service in New York and other places. The rest of the Terry-built ships were constructed as tow boats, ferries, and tug boats for use all along the Atlantic coast.

If it were not for the Civil War, the Terry shipbuilding era might have remained a remarkable but local story. With the advent of the war, the Federal Navy consisted of less than 20 seaworthy vessels ready for use; this included sailing ships. There were other vessels that had to be called in from distant parts of the world. The need was great for ships to move troops and supplies, to assist in blockading southern ports, to carry dispatches, and to take part in combat against Confederate ships. The government turned to Benjamin Terry among other ship builders and to owners of ships already in use. Before the war ended, 30 of the ships he had produced were either bought by the government or chartered for naval service. Two of his ships that had been sold earlier saw service in the Confederate Navy.

One of the earliest uses of Terry ships was for the Potomac Flotilla. With the Confederacy on one side of the Potomac and the Union on the other, and with Washington not far from Richmond, the Navy and War Departments recognized the need to protect our capital and blunt any significant buildups along the Virginia shores. Washington, at that time, was not served by railroads from the north, and the Confederacy hoped to cut it off from the rest of the country and even capture it. The *Reliance* and the *Resolute*, both Terry ships, were the first vessels bought to form the Flying Flotilla, later known as the Potomac Flotilla. The *Resolute* in two solo assignments captured and burned the schooner *Somerset* and landed a party of sailors to burn a Confederate supply depot.

On March 6, 1862, Terry's *Seth Low* started to tow the new Union ironclad *Monitor* from Sandy Hook to Hampton Roads for the famous battle between the *Monitor* and the *Merimac* (*Virginia*). Heavy seas were encountered during the tow, which broke over the deck of the *Monitor* and through vents and pipes to the boiler room. The little *Seth Low* managed to bring her ungainly burden to Hampton Roads, however, where history was made in the first battle of ironclads.

Terry's wooden side-wheel steam tug *Ceres* saw extensive service in the Federal Navy. After a brief service with the Potomac Flotilla, the *Ceres* was assigned to the Atlantic Blockading Squadron in September 1861. She participated in the capture of Roanoke Island in February 1862. Armament at first consisted of one 30-pounder

The battle between the Monitor *and the* Merrimac (Virginia).

rifle and a 32-pounder rifle, but by April 1863 she carried two 30-pounders and two 20-pounder Parrott rifles. After the capture of Roanoke Island, the *Ceres* was part of a fleet that pursued the Confederate fleet up the Pasquotank River. In that engagement, the *Ceres* captured the *C.S.S. Ellis* off Elizabeth City, North Carolina. In July 1862, she captured the Confederate steamer *Wilson*. In October 1863, she was sent to Mobjack Bay with four other vessels to break up a rebel unit called the Marine Coast Guard. In April 1864, the *Ceres* participated in a series of attacks around Plymouth, where she was frequently under fire from the guns at Fort Gray. Following these engagements, she took part in two attacks against the Confederate ram *Albemarle*. The *Albemarle* retired upriver, where she was sunk by a small torpedo boat. The *Ceres's* last duty was to tow the raised *Albemarle* to Norfolk, Virginia.

The most famous of the Terry ships to take part in the Civil War was the *River Queen*. She was launched in March 1864, and by December was chartered to the Army Quartermaster department. In January 1865, she was assigned to General Grant as his dispatch boat. On January 31, three Confederate peace commissioners came through the lines from Petersburg under a flag of truce. The *River Queen* was sent to Washington to take Secretary of State Seward to Fort Monroe, where he and General Grant began conferences with Confederate commissioners. During

Monmouth Marine Railway Company workers standing from left: F.P. Humphries (3rd), A. Andersen (4th), E. Cowell Sr (6th), Hancland (10th), R. Wernersen (12th), J. Jorgensen (13th), P. Hyer (14th), G. Smith (15th), P. Moy (18th), E. Erlandsen (19th), A. Jorgensen (20th), and J. Olsen (22nd). Kneeling from left: J. Adams (1st), E. Cowell Jr. (2nd), N. Andersen (3rd), N. Jacobsen (4th), T. Knutsen (5th), H. Cowell (8th), and G. Olsen (13th).

deliberations, Grant wired President Lincoln that he was needed to resolve certain matters under discussion. After the President arrived, he conferred with Seward until late into the night. Then the conference was moved to the *River Queen*. After four more hours of deliberation, they were at a stalemate, and the commissioners returned to the Confederacy.

The President and Secretary Seward then briefed General Grant at his headquarters ashore. The President and Seward then boarded the *River Queen* to sleep and return to Annapolis, and thence overland to Washington. On March 20, Grant invited the President to a conference with Generals Grant and Sherman and Admiral Porter and sent the *River Queen* to Washington to convey the President to the conference. On March 28, the President met with Grant, Sherman, and Porter in the after saloon of the *River Queen*. They discussed what measures could be taken to conclude the war. The President stayed aboard for several days. When he heard that Secretary Seward had been severely injured back in Washington, he decided to return there. The *River Queen* landed at Washington on March 9, and only days later on March 14, President Lincoln was assassinated at Ford Theater.

Thirty of the Terry vessels took part in the Civil War, and there are many other adventures in the war that could be recounted here. Instead, this author directs the reader's attention to *Steam Vessels Built in Old Monmouth 1841–1894* by Leon Reussille. There is no better authority on the subject.

Benjamin Terry continued to build steamships in Keyport after the war; the last one credited to him was the *Pleasant Valley* in 1870; about the same time it was said he was having marital problems. By 1876–1877, he pre-fabricated two ferry boats in Greenpoint, Brooklyn, and shipped them overland by train to San Francisco. Each ferry took 120 railroad flat cars to transport. In San Francisco, he supervised their assembly as the *San Rafael* and the *Sausalito*. Benjamin Terry never returned to the east coast.

Terry's failure to return, however, did not end ship building in Keyport. In 1875, five years after Terry's last Keyport boat, William L. Force built the *Ocean Gem*. She was built as a steam yacht with a length of 90 feet and weighed in at 74 tons, a very small vessel when compared with the Terry production. She was a graceful vessel, however, with a rounded stern, masts, and a bowsprit.

The last of the steamships built in Keyport was the *William V. Wilson*, which was built by James Wilson. The *Wilson* was 163 feet long and weighed 620 tons. It was really too large for the docking area of Compton's Creek, owned by the Middletown & Port Monmouth Steamboat Company, who also owned and operated the vessel. It was necessary to back out into the bay to turn around and head for New York. She was used chiefly as a market boat but also carried passengers.

During and since the days when Keyport's principal industry was building the first sailing ships and then steamships, there have been numerous boat builders. After the departure of Benjamin Terry, sons and other members of the Terry family turned to building boats at the Terry yards and elsewhere. The Terry yards changed hands several times, and by the 1920s, the Monmouth

Galbraith float and canoes. The building in the background was an oyster barge brought in by J. & J.W. Elsworth Company for opening oysters.

Marine Railway Company was producing boats of significance there. In 1920, they designed and built a power houseboat, the *Northwind* for Clarence Fisher of Red Bank. In 1925, they built the *Dobbins* for Harvey Dobbins of Red Bank, another power houseboat. In June 1928, Frederic Humphreys bought the yards and by October he was building the 72-foot yacht *Showboat* for Jerome Kern; the salon featured a built-in baby grand piano. Humphreys's last boat, 110-feet long, was along with the company a victim of the Depression. The boat lay in the building for ten years until the property was purchased by Arthur M. Gray, who sold the boat to a freight company in Norfolk. In 1940, the borough purchased the property.

Another boat builder became established by 1920 on the Luppatatong Creek at the bay. Hulgar "Marty" Kofoed had built fishing dories in Sea Bright prior to his move to Keyport. He was born on the Island of Bornholm in Denmark in 1888 and educated at the Denmark Academy of Naval Architecture. He worked his way to this country at 19 as a cook on the *Georg Stag*. By about 1910, he had established his first boat-building shop in Sea Bright. By 1920, he had married, had five sons, and had moved his boat-building operations to Keyport on the Luppatatong Creek. There are more details on his boatyard in the chapter on Prohibition, because he turned out a number of fine, fast sea skiffs used by rum runners during that era. Kofoed, by 1946, as a representative of the Richardson Boat Company, had announced a new design with a molded mahogany hull. By 1948, however, his boatyard was sold at sheriff's sale to Galbraith & Son.

Galbraith had been in business in Keyport since before 1917, when their plant at Broad and Maple Place burned. Their primary business was lifeboats and life-saving equipment. They had leased the property of J. & J.W. Ellsworth [now Firemen's Park] in 1936 and produced a huge luxury yacht for a wealthy sugar baron. In 1939, they purchased the Tingley Rubber Company building on Manchester Avenue. They continued operation there into the 1950s.

Hans Pedersen learned the boat-building business in Denmark during World War I. He followed his brother August to this country in 1929 and worked in the Humphreys yard until it closed. In 1937, he started his own boat business first on Second Street and then at the waterfront at Prospect Street, but it closed down in 1941 when his sons and sons-in-law went into service. After the war, his brother August died, and he took over the business as Hans Pedersen & Sons and moved to Highway 36. His son-in-law Andrew Ulrichsen started his own company. Pedersen moved his operations to the old Hensler-Kofoed yard and built a new shop in 1962. He and his sons Ivan and Eric built many sleek cabin cruisers there over the years until in the 1970s wooden boats went out of fashion. They still refurbish boats with fine mahogany and build the occasional wooden boat along with running a yacht harbor.

A lifeboat produced by Galbraith at its bayshore plant.

7. Those Oysters, Those Fortunes

Oysters are grown commercially on beds of shells. Unlike the clam, the oyster cannot survive when buried. The oysterman plants seed oysters on staked out beds and then harvests them three to four years later. Seed oysters originate in spawn carried by the tides. The spawn contains untold numbers of spats, which attach themselves to rocks or shells on the bottom.

Keyport oystermen brought seed oysters from Newark Bay in the mid-1800s, but soon went to the Chesapeake Bay exclusively as a source. At Chesapeake Bay, the oysterman would hoist an empty oyster basket to the top of the mast, and those who gathered the seed oysters would flock to him in small boats. An oyster planter would return to the Raritan Bay with typically 2,500 to 3,000 bushels of seed oysters. He would sail back and forth across his designated beds, where fresh shells had been strewn in preparation, and scatter shovels of seed oysters on top of the shells. The beds would extend for several acres.

After the oyster had grown to maturity—usually about 3 years—the oystermen would either tong or, more often, dredge them from the beds shells and all (sometimes they would grow in a cluster) into the boats. They would be piled into oyster baskets and taken by small scows to the Luppatatong Creek, where the baskets would be lined up in the creek for "drinking" at low tide. Drinking refers to the process oysters use to cleanse themselves when placed in a stream of clean water. One oyster can take in 50 gallons of water a day and purify it. This allowed water to wash through the oysters and plump them up. They would then be raised into the oyster houses, where men would open them into 1- to 5-gallon cans. The cans would be packed in ice in tubs and shipped to market.

In 1718, an act was passed for the Preserving of Oysters in the Province of New Jersey. Thomas Kearney, John Bowne, Robert Carhart, Abraham Watson, and Richard Brittain were appointed commissioners for the County of Monmouth. Kearney had bought what is now Keyport from John Bowne in 1714. In the plantation years following, oysters were planted and gathered in Luppatatong Creek and were referred to as Chingarora oysters; the Chingarora is another creek farther east along the Keyport waterfront.

After the Orphan's Court sale and establishment of Keyport, in 1840 a number of men from Staten Island saw the possibilities of earning a great fortune in oystering on the sheltered coast of Keyport. In the early and mid-1800s, oysters were eaten primarily by the wealthy except for people in the local areas where they were grown. Captain Peter Metsgar was one of the first to come from Staten Island to Keyport for this purpose. He was at a time one of the largest planters in the bay, putting down as much as $50,000 of seed oyster in a season. Captains Jacob and Benjamin Decker arrived shortly after and engaged in oyster planting on a grand scale.

Captain Cornelius Britton came to Keyport in 1844 and became the best known and biggest oyster planter in the state. He employed scores of men, was associated with many of the large dealers in New York, and controlled a great part of the industry in Keyport. Several other oyster planters followed.

March 1860 marked the first and bloodiest crime to ever occur on the oyster boats. On March 18, the oyster sloop *E.A. Johnson* sailed from Keyport headed for Islip, Long Island. On March 21, 1860, three men rowing off Staten Island saw the *E.A. Johnson* drifting with no signs of life aboard. They rowed to the boat, called, and then climbed aboard. The sails were torn and hanging over the side, and the deck was in shambles. On the sails, mast, stove, and companion

Drinking oysters in Luppatatong Creek to plump them up.

hatch was blood. It seemed to be all over, but not a soul was aboard. Boxes and chests were hacked open. The three men towed the sloop to the nearest port and notified the authorities. After some time passed, the authorities found a member of the crew named Hicks who had left Keyport on March 18 and was discovered in a lodging house in New York with the captain's watch and other articles. He admitted killing the three others aboard and looting the bodies and vessel. He claimed the "devil" urged him to commit the crime, but he was publicly executed on July 13, 1860.

An Oyster Planters Association was established on January 28, 1882, with T.S.R. Brown as president, Captain Peter Metsgar vice president, G. Morris Britton secretary, and S.B. Cubberly treasurer. In that year, over 80 prominent men in Keyport were engaged in the oyster industry. Many invested their earnings in real estate and others in Keyport businesses. In the 1880–1881 season, 70,768 barrels of oysters were shipped from this country to Europe. In the same season, $150,000 of seed oysters were planted in Raritan Bay, and the export of shellfish alone brought $500,000. Almost the entire output from Keyport went to the New York market, but Keyport's Chingarora oyster also went to San Francisco, Los Angeles, Denver, and Salt Lake City. By about 1880, the plentiful supply of oysters made consumer prices lower than for meat, poultry, and fish, thus oysters were eaten by people at all economic levels.

In June 1899, the J. & J.W. Elsworth Company began to erect its plant in Keyport and opened for business the same month on the edge of Luppatatong

Shucking oysters inside the Elsworth oyster house.

Creek. The home office was at West Washington Market in New York. They had oyster farms at Oyster Bay, Greenport, Jessup Neck, North Lea, Sag Harbour, Rockaway, South Norwalk, and Great Kills. At times, oysters were brought to Keyport from all of these farms in their very large fleet of fast vessels, thus there was an early need for a dock to service the Keyport operation. In 1903, they were able to buy the coal dock of the Burrowes Brothers but had to buy the coal business too. Thereafter, they were in the coal business as well.

On a typical day, oyster boats would go out to the beds and lower overboard great dredges that would hold about 8 bushels. They would then drag the bottom going at about half speed until these dredges were full. They would then haul the dredges aboard using the power of the engines. Men on board would sort them and put them into baskets holding 5 pecks. At the plant, after "drinking" the baskets of oysters, they would be shucked using great quantities of water to keep everything scrupulously clean. The Elsworth Company marketed their oysters as the Red Cross brand and shipped them as far away as Japan. They were to become the largest oyster company in the country.

The year 1900 opened with announcements that Captain William E. Woolley had started south for seed oysters. The schooner *Flora Kirwan* arrived with 2,000 tubs for Thomas C. Mason, and the Lorena Clayton arrived with 2,500 bushels for Mason Brothers. Also, several men were employed in opening oysters at Elsworth's, and some barreled oysters were being shipped to Philadelphia. Then came the mystery. Captain James Baldwin of Keyport had been buying oysters and clams locally and then carrying them up the Hudson River to markets as far as Albany. He stopped at the city of Hudson to buy supplies. His body was then found in the water near his vessel minus the $300 he had with him. He had been robbed of $200 two years before.

In April 1901, the Clammers Protective Association decided to commence work on the oyster beds of Garrett B. Post, claiming his was really a natural oyster and clamming ground. Natural oyster beds are those that occur naturally without prior planting of seed oysters; they are open to anyone. Mr. Post claimed the beds had been in his undisputed possession for 17 years, and under law, undisputed possession for 10 years secures the exclusive right to plant and harvest oysters. He acquired an injunction against the clammers and, when they persisted, had 16 of them arrested. Despite arrests and injunctions, the clammers continued to harvest oysters.

In the first few months of 1903, the State Oyster Commission recommended and the legislature passed a law regulating oystering and clamming. The state was divided into three districts, the northern one running from Barnegat Bay to Jersey City. The State Oyster Commission met at the Mansion House in Keyport on April 22 and decided that before receiving any lease applications for oyster grounds, they would have Raritan Bay surveyed. The land reserved for planting in Keyport was about 2 square miles and was delineated as follows:

> Beginning at the watch house at Connasconk point, on the shore of Raritan Bay; thence on a straight line to the government buoy, known

Oyster barges on the Hudson River used as the New York market before the Fulton Market opened.

> as East Point buoy; thence on a true course west south west to the point where said course intersects a line drawn on a course due north from Cliffwood point; thence along the shore line to the place of beginning.

In the previous year, about 800 acres were leased. The law provided for the maintenance of a watch boat. On July 19, 1903, Sharp & Sharp of Bridgeton, New Jersey, contracted to survey the oyster grounds of Raritan Bay. The survey was completed by the end of July.

In May 1903, Keyport watermen discovered a very large natural deposit of clams. At first, only Asbury Bedle knew of it; he worked nights and brought in very large quantities. Then a few saw he was doing well and watched where he went; they worked only at night and told no one. Finally the secret could no longer be kept and a huge crowd descended on the site, which was depleted in a week.

Headlines in the Newark papers in November announced that an oyster from Raritan Bay had been found with green spots and an astringent taste. It was felt this was from contact with copper in the water from copper wastes dumped into the water by the Raritan Copper Works Company and the

Guggenheim Smelting Company in Perth Amboy. The *Newark Evening News* suggested in an editorial that the state board of health take action to stop the dumping. The oystermen's reaction was that this instance was nothing new and occurred rarely.

In May 1904, J. & J.W. Elsworth Company decided to bring oysters from all of their grounds to Keyport for drinking in the pure waters of Luppatatong Creek. It is interesting to note that since establishing the Elsworth Company on this creek, it has been known popularly as "Oyster Creek." Also in May, the Company shipped 200 carloads of seed oysters, amounting to 84,000 bushels, to the Morgan Oyster Company in San Francisco. The cargo was so perishable that each one had to be iced six times en route. Of the 200 carloads sent, 7 were from Keyport harbor. On August 30, the company shipped out 300,000 oysters, mostly to Philadelphia, the largest amount they ever shipped in one day. On October 30, 1904, the *New York Tribune Illustrated* supplement ran an extensive article with pictures of the J. & J.W. Elsworth Company and its operations.

Since 1890, the New York market for oysters had been in a string of oyster barges in a basin along the Hudson River between the fish dock at the foot of Beekman Street and Pier 24. In November 1904, a big dredge was pushed into the basin and tugs towed away the oyster barges. This was the first step in establishing an enlarged Fulton Fish Market as the new market for oysters as well as all other seafood.

In 1905, the Elsworth Company nearly doubled the size of the oyster house by building out over the creek. The street or north side became a storage area, and the creek side became the area for opening oysters. During the season, about 100 barrels were shipped daily to Philadelphia. The Oyster Act was amended in the same year to establish severe penalties for dredging or tonging on lands leased under the act without permission from the lessee.

In 1906, a number of Keyporters employed in the Elsworth Company went to South Norwalk, Connecticut, to work. The company closed its doors in September for the season because the openers went on strike. They had been paying 20¢ per measure for opening oysters. The measure was supposed to hold a gallon, but really held 5 quarts; in addition, there was a lip to the measure, which held about another quart. At first, there was some grumbling about the size of the cup, but it blew over. The company then brought in two Connecticut openers, who turned out to be labor agitators. The workers walked off demanding that the lip be removed. One of the agitators, Lee Earl, stayed and worked all day. There was a great deal of anger, and a constable had to be called in to protect him. Despite the presence of an officer, the crowd seized Earl and threw him into the creek. All orders were canceled, and only barrels of unopened oysters were shipped out for that season. For 1906, 117 boats used in the oyster trade were licensed, and 593.25 acres were leased in the bay—a decrease of 136.75 acres.

In April 1907, James L. Hammer bought a schooner-load of seed oysters in Hampton Bar, Virginia. While there, he and former chief Woolley visited the

Oyster barges behind the Elsworth house. Baskets of oysters were hauled up from the barges for shucking.

grounds of the Jamestown Exposition, which was under construction. They looked for the New Jersey building but could not find it. In April 1908, a member of the New York State Oyster Commission took samples of oysters from Raritan Bay beds, including Keyport. There had been outbreaks of typhoid, and it was thought that oysters were the cause. Thorough testing proved no relationship. In July 1908, Abram and Forman Smith of Keyport were apprehended for taking oysters from Frederick E. Post's grounds. Hendrick Poling and Jacob Decker, watchmen for the Oyster Planters Association, testified as witnesses. Both culprits were fined $50 and costs. The Elsworth Company was back in operation but with only 50 men employed. Manager Van Buskirk reported that the season was not as good as it could have been.

For some time, a number of local watermen had been gathering natural oysters and for lack of a market, had been throwing them out along the shore, waiting for a chance to sell at a decent price. In September 1908, the Elsworth Company offered them 50¢ per bushel, take it or leave it. Among those holding oysters were Captain Eugene Decker of the *Ida Virginia*, Captain John Kipp of the *Delghinia*, Captain James Kipp of the *Thomas Collins*, Captain Daniel Decker of the *Hagerman*, and Captain Charles Burlew of the *Lydia Van Name*. To their surprise, when they went to their boats on September 23, they each found a note, "Anybody selling their oysters for 50¢ a bushel will lose their boat and tools." The writer was never discovered, and the threat did not phase the oystermen.

The process of drinking oysters was in contention in a hearing before the Secretary of Agriculture in Washington in March 1910. The Pure Food Commission had ruled against the practice, but 200 New Jersey men from the industry attended the hearing and presented their case. The decision rendered in June was that drinking oysters would be permitted, but they must be so labeled. All of this hit home when the Elsworth Company had the water of Luppatatong Creek tested and found it to be contaminated by sewer drains. On September 9, the company threatened to pull out of Keyport if nothing was done to improve conditions. The warning must have been taken seriously, because at a special election on September 14, a majority of the people of Keyport voted to build a sanitary sewer system.

Keyport oyster planters and the acreage leased by each were listed in the April 15, 1910 issue of the *Keyport Weekly*. They were: Walter S. Birkbeck with 17 acres, William DeGroff with 57.5 acres, Hammer & Son with 42.25 acres, John W. Mason with 14.75 acres, Lorenzo G. Mason with 35 acres, William Maurer with 81.5 acres, Garret E. Post with 91.75 acres, and William E. Woolley with 157.5 acres. The Elsworth Company was not listed because its headquarters were in New York.

A state law was passed on April 6 calling for annual (or more often) inspection of oyster grounds by the State Board of Health. The board had the right to

The large "building" in the background is an oyster barge brought in by J. & J.W. Elsworth for shucking oysters.

condemn any grounds if found to be polluted and prohibit the gathering of oysters therefrom.

In July, the Elsworth Company sent large quantities of shells from Keyport to its grounds in Bridgeport and New Haven, Connecticut. One of the William Foster Company's large oyster scows was tied up at its dock for use as a facility to open oysters, thus enabling an expansion of the work force. Many of the openers on the barge were imported from the Seaford area of Delaware. In March of 1915, the oyster scow was made a permanent part of the operation by placing it behind the bulkhead on solid ground.

The year ended with two cases brought before the courts for taking oysters from an established oyster bed. In the first case, John Ansbro was charged with taking oysters while raking clams. A witness testified that there were no oysters in the bed, only oyster shells and Mr. Ansbro was acquitted. In the second case, Charles Heyer Sr. was convicted of raking clams in the oyster bed of William Maurer and fined $50 plus costs.

More than 100,000 gallons of oysters were opened and shipped from the Elsworth Company during the 1910–1911 season. New Jersey declared the week of October 20–25 as Oyster Week and the state printed and distributed a booklet of recipes for oysters so they could be eaten in many ways. John W. Elsworth of J. & J.W. Elsworth Company died on March 15, 1916. Joseph E. Elsworth, the senior member of the firm, died several years before. J.W. was survived by his widow, a brother Robert, and a sister Jennie.

Charges of discrimination by New York authorities against New Jersey oyster planters in Raritan Bay were made on April 4, 1916, by Senator Henry E. Ackerson Jr., of Keyport. He was appearing as counsel for a number of oystermen in the Keyport area. The oysters had been accepted by the New Jersey Health Board and federal authorities. It appeared at the time that New York was discriminating against New Jersey in order to promote the business of New York oystermen. In August 1917, representatives of the State Oyster Commission and several local oystermen made an inspection of the grounds. One of the purposes of the inspection was to locate any barren grounds. J. & J.W. Elsworth had been shipping many freight car loads of shells to Barnegat Bay to promote oyster production there. In April 1917, the Elsworth Company offered its entire fleet of boats to the Naval reserve. The offer was accepted and all 21 boats were enrolled in the reserve.

In June 1919, there was a widespread protest against the pollution of Raritan Bay by industrial plants on the Raritan River and along Staten Island. There were fish kills along the shores and bathers broke out in rashes. The authorities, both federal and state, were unable to take any effective action. An oyster bill was proposed in March 1920 to "give back" the oyster grounds to individuals, because large industries were in control of most of the oyster grounds. One concern was that men returning from the war were not able to obtain oyster leases.

In November 1925, the State Board of Health banned the taking of all oysters and clams in Raritan Bay and Sandy Hook Bay. The effect on both industries was devastating. Again the companies on the Raritan River and along the Staten Island shore were blamed along with the effluents of sewer plants from cities and towns. The ban continued for ten years. In October 1935, New York City lifted its ban on oysters and clams from New Jersey, but in February 1936, the federal government banned all interstate shipment of oysters and clams from New Jersey. In April 1936, J. & J.W. Elsworth Company closed its doors in Keyport. Several employees accepted jobs with the Greenport, Long Island, branch of the company and the Keyport holdings of the Elsworth Company were leased to the Galbraith Company for their boat-building and life-saving equipment business. Thus ended an industry in Keyport and all of the Raritan Bay communities that employed many people, made many fortunes, and fed people as far away as Europe and Japan.

Oyster boats and oyster shacks near the mouth of Luppatatong Creek.

8. From Disaster: A Fire Department

By 1877, Keyport was a thriving seaport with docks, warehouses, stores, hotels, and stables in the business district. On September 21, 1877, at 11 p.m., a group of National Guardsmen were on their way home from a meeting when they saw flames erupt from the rear of A. Morris's market located on the west side of Broad Street midway between Front and First Streets, where the Monmouth Lounge was located later. They rushed to the fire and then, realizing that saving the building was impossible and that adjoining buildings were in danger, they spread the alarm. There was no fire department in Keyport and no central water system. People poured into the streets to help battle the blaze, and since there was no fire apparatus, they formed bucket brigades starting at the edge of Raritan Bay. By this means, The Pavilion Hotel (later the Raritan Inn) and an adjacent grocery store located at the top of the hill on the east side of Broad Street were saved from the conflagration.

The rest of the business district, however, was beyond preservation. The Mansion House, located on the northeast corner of Front and Broad Streets, was burned to the ground. From this point, the flames spread eastward on the north side of Front Street to the foot of the hill. They then jumped Front Street and raced up the hill toward Broad Street destroying every building, including the Episcopal Church, the law offices of Judge Walling, and the drug store owned by Dr. E. McKinney. All of the structures were built of wood.

Crossing Broad Street, the fire then attacked the general store of Block & Salz on the southwest corner of Front and Broad and continued westward on Front Street to the alley that now leads to the borough parking lot. Meanwhile, everything on the north side of Front Street had been wiped out from Broad Street to where the Bulkhead Restaurant now stands. Broad Street, south of Front, was swept on both sides to where the Broad Street entrance to the borough parking lot is located today. A feed store stood on the west side of the street. The fire fighters, using bucket brigades, concentrated on the building and extinguished the flames, but hours later the flames rekindled and the building was consumed. Not a structure in the area described was spared.

Devastation from the great fire of 1877 looking northeast toward the Pavilion Hotel, which was saved.

The fire department from Matawan arrived at about 1 p.m. in response to a call for aid and fought valiantly to check the flames. However, the fire had reached such proportions that their apparatus, a hand pumper, was inadequate to cope with the raging inferno. The entire town appeared to be doomed. Suddenly, a providential thing happened. The wind, which had been blowing furiously, shifted to the southwest and then died out completely. It was this sudden and miraculous shift that saved the town from destruction and led to the end of the conflagration.

Company G of the Third New Jersey Guards, under the command of Captain Ben Lee, was called out early in the evening, and the town was placed under military rule. Forty-two posts were established throughout the town, and no one was allowed to enter or leave the stricken area without good cause. In spite of their vigilance, a great deal of looting was reported. It was even said that wagons arrived and carted away much plunder left unguarded.

An area opposite Beers Street along the bay was then a park. Goods from the burning buildings were brought to the park and placed under guard. This procedure, to a large degree, put an end to the widespread looting.

It was 5 a.m. before the fire had been completely extinguished. Approximately 35 buildings and hundreds of thousands of dollars' worth of property had been

Devastation from the great fire of 1877 looking east. The Salz store was completely destroyed.

destroyed. Considering the comparative value of money, the same damage today would have been in the millions. The dawn of September 23, 1877, presented a scene of desolate ruin.

Shortly after this fateful day, many of the prominent men met in the F.D. Woodruff building on the south side of Front Street and planned the organization of the first fire company. Thus, on October 10, 1877, Hook & Ladder Company Number 1 came into existence. The first home of Hook & Ladder was a building on the northwest corner of Cross (now Third) and Broad Streets. It was also used by the town commissioners for their meetings until 1886, when a brick structure was erected by W.A. Tilton at the present site of Terry's Tees on East Front Street across from the corner of Osborn Street. In 1986, Hook & Ladder Company and Engine Company Number 1 merged to form Consolidated Fire Company. In 1921, the Ladies Auxiliary of Hook & Ladder was formed. Their support in raising funds for the company was a significant factor, but those hot cups of coffee provided to all firemen at fires on cold, wintry nights over the years were what endeared them to the entire department.

On July 18, 1889, 15 men gathered at the Keyport Athletic Club on First Street (now Beach Park) to organize Keyport's second fire company. From 1877 to then, the only fire equipment available was a ladder truck carrying two dozen leather buckets. It was decided a hose apparatus was needed in town for fighting fires, and the town commissioners were asked to obtain a hose apparatus. While a chemical engine was on order, on November 28, 1889, a second terrible fire struck the

Keyport business section. It started in a bakery, destroyed seven buildings, and damaged others. There was one fatality, even though Keyport received assistance from the Matawan and Red Bank fire departments. There was no water system and only one fire company with an apparatus in town. The insurance companies threatened higher rates unless Keyport invested in fire equipment and a central water system. The apparatus for Keyport Engine Company was received in October 1890 and was placed in rooms of the Keyport Athletic Club. The company purchased a lot on Main Street in 1891 and issued bonds to build a firehouse. George Washington Walling, former chief of police for New York, was elected trustee and the cornerstone was laid in July 1891. The apparatus, a chemical wagon, was pulled by hand and later at times by hitching a tow from a "horseless carriage."

The year 1893 saw three more fire companies added to the department. On March 31, 1893, a group of men met in the sail loft at the Terry Ship Yard to organize a hose company for the Lockport section of Keyport. S.P. Dey was

Hook & Ladder Fire Company, the first fire department. The building also served as a Town Hall.

chosen chairman of the meeting, E.S. Walling president, and M.L. Terry secretary. The name chosen for the new company was the American Hose Company, but this was later changed to Lincoln Hose Company Number 1. In 1953, Lincoln purchased the former Smith Lumber Company, renovated the building, and moved to its present location on Second Street.

Perhaps rallying to the call that "everyone couldn't be No. 1," Raritan Hose Company Number 2 was the second company formed in 1893. Captain Asbury F. Bedle, Alfred Cuttrell, Richard S. White, and other members of Company G, 3rd Regiment, National Guard of New Jersey, met at the Armory on First Street to form a new hose company. At a formal meeting on May 29, officers were elected and plans made for suitable equipment. The horse-drawn apparatus obtained shortly thereafter was housed in the company room of the armory. At its inception, Raritan Hose admitted only military men. This changed with time, but for a long while military discipline was maintained within the company. Raritan Hose paraded in uniforms of long grey coats and fire helmets.

George W. Birch Jr. joined Raritan Hose in December 1907 after serving with Hook & Ladder. He remained an active member until his death in 1963. He served as secretary of the company for 50 of those years and as secretary of the Firemen's Relief Association as well. In the early part of 1900, the Company built a firehouse on Division Street and, two years later, purchased a lot on Broad

Raritan Hose Number 2 in their parade uniforms featuring the long gray coats. George Birch is fourth from the left.

Street near the northwest corner of Third, and moved the fire house to the new location. In 1968, Raritan purchased property on the corner of Church Street and Maple Place. In June 1969, the members started clearing the land. This author's father-in-law, Peter LaMonte, cleared the lush growth of poison ivy with his bare hands (he wasn't allergic to it).

The building committee, under the guiding hand of William G. Newman, organized the construction and, by October 1969, Raritan Hose moved into its new quarters. In 1973, with a change in the borough ordinance lowering the age for joining the fire department, Raritan Hose enrolled Robert T. Jeandron as the first 18-year old active fireman in the department.

The third company to organize in 1893 was Liberty Hose Company Number 3. It was organized and incorporated on June 30 largely through the efforts of James W. Holmes, a member of Engine Company Number 1, and Alvarado M. Walling, a member of Hook & Ladder. They called a meeting of the men of south Keyport at the offices of the Theodore Aumack Carriage Factory, where the company was formed with 14 charter members. Their first home was a one-story fire house in July 1893 on Atlantic Street near where it joins South Main Street. In May 1939, the company purchased property at the southwest corner of Atlantic Street and Route 36. In 1948, the company built a new firehouse there and later built its present house on the same property.

Until 1907, all parts of Keyport had established fire companies except Brown's Point. Through the urging of Alfred Geran and others, a meeting was held on June 17, 1907, in Harry P. Disbrow's bottling establishment. It resulted in the organization of Eagle Hose Company Number 4, and the charter members selected William Sieben as foreman, Judson Hopla as president, Granville Disbrow as secretary, and Harry P. Disbrow as treasurer. The first firehouse was a barn on the Hopla property on Broadway rented for $5 per month with cost of remodeling credited toward rent. The barn was remodeled to provide a truck room in front and a meeting room in the rear. In January 1911, a lot on Broadway near the corner of West First Street was purchased for a new firehouse, and the company was incorporated. The new firehouse was started in November 1912 and completed in March 1913.

The Keyport Board of Fire Wardens originally was composed of 12 men, two of whom were selected from each of the six fire companies. The ordinance of 1910, however, provided for a fire patrol as a separate company. The first patrol after the 1910 ordinance was formed with former mayor William L. Latham as chief and meetings were held at members' houses. Mr. Latham served as chief until 1924, when he resigned. Fire patrol's first vehicle (in 1926) was a Ford truck and the equipment on it included a lung motor, so it was pressed into service as a First Aid ambulance. This was prior to formation of the First Aid Squad in Engine Company. Fire patrol had no residence and rented various garages around town, one of which was Schanck's garage at Broad and Third Streets. In 1933, they rented space from Lincoln Hose Company in its firehouse on Waverly Street. In 1953, when Lincoln moved to its new firehouse, fire patrol purchased the Waverly Street firehouse from Lincoln. This was expanded in 1972 to accommodate the new truck, the building was brick-coated, and adjoining land was purchased.

The first fire alarm of the Keyport Fire Department was a locomotive wheel rim presented to the department by an official of the New York & Long Branch Railroad Company. It was first mounted by the Hook & Ladder fire house on the northwest corner of Broad and Cross (now Third) Streets. It was later moved to First Street near Broad Street and has since disappeared.

After Hook & Ladder moved to the building on East Front Street, it purchased a bell and presented it to the town. It was used until it was replaced by the Gamewell box system. The bell is now displayed at Firemen's Park on Front Street near Luppatatong Creek. The disadvantage of earlier alarms was that they did not indicate the location of the fire. Through the efforts of Ernest Bailey, then a member of the council, a Gamewell fire alarm system was installed and placed in service December 23, 1923. This system used fire alarm boxes placed strategically throughout the borough for triggering a centrally-located horn. The number indicated by the blasts of the horn provided the location of the alarm box. It was commonly called the "cow" because it sounded very much like one.

In the 1970s, so many false alarms were sounded from fire alarm boxes that the borough discontinued their use as telephone calls to the police department became the substitute. Police headquarters sounded the alarm using the same "cow" with a limited numbering system, then sent out a signal to individual firemen over a silent Plectron system. In the Plectron system, each fireman is given a pager linked to a central sending device at Police Headquarters. When the police receive a fire call, they send out a page to all firemen.

There is a record of first aid calls answered during 1926 by volunteers in Keyport. This, however, was before formal steps were taken to organize as a First Aid Squad. The Keyport First Aid Squad organized on November 2, 1927, at Engine Company as part of the fire department. A first aid class was organized using American Red Cross standards of instruction, and the squad continued to answer calls using private cars and a fire truck. The equipment was meager, consisting of first aid kits, splints, blankets, a stretcher, and an inhalator. A successful resuscitation was performed on one of their first emergencies.

Their first ambulance was a 1928 Meteor, financed by a fund drive in Keyport and surrounding areas. In a short time, they were providing first aid service for an area extending from South Amboy to Atlantic Highlands and areas bounded by Old Bridge, Marlboro, Colts Neck, and Red Bank. The nearest hospitals were South Amboy and Red Bank, with many calls going to Monmouth Memorial and Hazard Hospitals in Long Branch.

With such an extensive area to cover, many members supplemented their training to qualify as instructors. They then trained others in the area, which led to the formation of squads in other towns around.

In 1927 or 1928, the Keyport First Aid left the fire department and incorporated as a separate entity. They purchased a building at 118 Broad Street (where Jesus the Lord RC Church is today) and converted it to house the ambulance and provide a meeting room. In September 1967, they moved into a modern three-bay building on Atlantic Street with a large meeting hall in the rear of the building.

In 1962, three members of the First Aid, William Ralph, Tony Senk, and Frank Fleming, wrote to Dr. Claude S. Beck in Ohio who had been researching the use of heart massage to save those whose hearts had stopped. Most of the research had been with animals. The Keyport First Aid men were invited to go to the laboratory to learn this new technology. When they returned, they applied the techniques of external heart massage successfully and set up a program to teach other first aid squads. The use of external heart massage is now widespread, but the Keyport First Aid was the pioneer squad.

Eagle Hose in 1907 posing with a hose cart.

9. The Horse Cars and Jersey Central Traction

The Keyport and Matawan Street Railway incorporated on July 7, 1887. It included a group of four from New York who were in the business of supplying streetcars and equipment. The other five involved were local men who had tried to establish a horse-drawn railroad earlier. Work on building the line began in earnest by July 16, with track being laid on First Street starting at Walnut Street and the erection of a car barn and offices in an area on the northwest corner of Broadway and what became Route 35. Six passenger cars were purchased and 40 horses.

By August 1887, the bridge was being widened across the gully by the gas house (essentially where the Garden State Parkway goes under Lower Main Street in Aberdeen), Italian labor was being brought in, and 250,000 bricks were purchased from Robbin's yard for the construction of the stables and car houses (barns) at Browns Point.

On Wednesday, September 21, the first car for the street railway arrived on the steamship *Holmdel*. The car was built by John Stephenson of New York "in the most improved and substantial manner, with all the latest conveniences including patent springs which add to the comfort of passengers." Theodore R. Thorne of Holmdel had the contract to supply 36 horses for the company; when the first car arrived, he brought down four of them. They were hitched to the car, and it was put through its paces on the completed section on First Street. Children were allowed to ride free on the first day, and on the next day several of the directors and two members of the press were paraded down First Street. John W. Walling, Benjamin Smith, John Young, and J.D. Williamson were hired as drivers for the street cars; J.D. Williamson did the inaugural drive, and John Hill was the first to pay a fare on the Keyport street cars.

The grand opening was held on October 3, 1887, three months after incorporation, with a huge extravaganza. There were flags and buntings everywhere, a large sum had been raised for refreshments, a grand arch covered with evergreens and flags spanned Broad and Front Streets with a sign "Welcome All," and fireworks and the sound of cannons filled the air. The procession moved from Walnut along First Street to Broad, thence up the hill and west on Front, across Lupatatong Creek to Broadway, past the new car barns, up Maple Place past the Catholic Church, across the bridge by the gas house, and to the end of the line before the tracks by the railroad station in Matawan. There were many speeches following the procession, and the day concluded with hundreds of bushels of clams from a huge clam pit at the Pavilion Hotel and a concert by the 69th Regiment Band at Walling Hall.

After all of this fanfare, the Keyport and Matawan Street Railway proceeded to provide a regular service along its line. The Blizzard of 1888 hit less than a year after service started and provided considerable challenges. The company worked its way through it and went on to meet its schedules and carry a large load of traffic. However, there were financial problems, and the line went into foreclosure on March 20, 1890, at the Keyport Town Hall. For a bid of $5, John Keough became the new owner and reorganized as The Keyport and Matawan Street Railroad Company.

The new company was capitalized at $50,000 and included the turnpike between Keyport and Matawan as part of its operation. The cars on the line were double-ended; when one reached the end of the line, the horses were unhitched and moved to the other end of the car for the return trip. The company reduced the number of horses and hitched only two to a trolley. The new company continued the tradition of providing efficient on-time service. Other events were closing in on horse car systems, however. Elsewhere trolleys were beginning to run on electric power.

In January 1898, the Township Board of Commissioners considered the application for the street railroad company to change from horse power to electric power. Keyport wanted, as part of the package, to have the roads paved and gain some electricity for lighting. However, they were unable to accomplish this under the franchise already in place, and permission was granted.

The horse trolley in front of the old car barns on Broadway near Six Corners.

The company engaged the East Jersey Power Company to measure for the trolley lines throughout town. It contracted for poles with D. Lane Conover and started installing them, and work on laying new rails started on May 31, 1901. On Decoration Day, the last horse car ran over the line with a banner on its side stating there would be no more cobble rides. A. Salz & Company had the contract for uniforms for the conductors and motormen. Working night and day, the tracks were laid from the eastern end of the line to Broadway and Front Street, and the one car in service carried a total of 775 passengers on July 4 and additional cars were added in the next two weeks. Ironically, one of the horses from the street railway was frightened by one of the trolleys and Superintendent Washabaugh was dumped unceremoniously from the carriage.

The town commissioners granted a new trolley franchise in August that called for a 5¢ fare to Matawan Station. On Labor Day, the trolley carried large crowds and there were waiting lines of up to 100 people. William Wheeler was riding on the step of an open trolley while it was crossing Oyster (Luppatatong) Creek and struck part of the bridge, but luckily he escaped with only a torn coat. Nathan Brewer was not so fortunate; at the same spot, while riding on the step, he was thrown to the ground and bruised badly. The dynamo on one of the trolleys broke down and put the line out of service for days in mid-September.

The company was granted a franchise by Raritan (now Hazlet) Township to extend the line eastward to the Middletown line. In October 1901, the Keyport and Matawan Railroad Company became the Jersey Central Traction Company (JCT). The principal owner was the East Jersey Power and Light Company. In May of 1902, JCT offered for sale the turnpike leading between Keyport and Matawan Station.

The generator at the powerhouse burned out on May 17 and was still not repaired on June 6 of 1902; the *Keyport Weekly* wrote a scathing editorial on May

Trolleys of Jersey Central Traction Company meeting a ship arriving at the Keyport docks.

30 and again on August 22. JCT filed a survey for an extension of the line to Red Bank going through "Keansburgh," Atlantic Highlands, and New Monmouth in July 1902. Two new vestibule cars were received in October and four more at the end of October equipped with nine cane seats, holding two on each side with a center aisle. The motor burned out in one of the cars while on the Broad Street hill.

Three lighters arrived at the Keyport docks in November 1902 loaded with T-rails for the trolley line between Keyport and South Amboy, and between Keyport and Red Bank. However, approvals for laying that track would not soon be forthcoming. By March 1903, however, the company was having the Cliffwood drawbridge rebuilt by the New Jersey Bridge Company, and Keyport had adopted an ordinance allowing JCT to lay tracks from Broadway and Bridge Street (West Front Street) to Matawan Creek.

JCT was sued for $10,000 by George Spires of Cheesequake, who was almost killed by a sagging live wire. He was returning to his home from South Amboy when his horse fell to the ground, so he left the carriage to investigate and came into contact with the wire. The jury awarded him $3,283 in addition to doctor's bills.

JCT ordered six new trolley cars of the latest design from Niles, Ohio, in June of 1903. When they were delivered on August 24 and 25, they were described as handsome, with the same facilities and appearance as "steam railroad cars." They even had bars on the windows to prevent riders from protruding their heads out the windows and coming into contact with bridge railings, etc., along the line. Each car was divided into two compartments, one for smokers, and each car had a toilet.

A war started in July of 1903 between JCT and the Central Railroad Company about JCT crossing the railroad right of way. When JCT would try to lay tracks to cross over, the railroad would pull up a few engines and block them. When JCT managed to run wires over the right of way, the railroad people would throw ropes over them, pull them down, and sever them. Finally, JCT went to the chancellor requesting a restraining order against the railroad. All of this occurred at Newtown (Union Beach) near the car barns at Florence Avenue and Broadway. While the two companies battled, JCT built a bridge at Lorillard (Natco Ponds) and ran the line to the Waackaack Creek. In addition, JCT managed to get one car across the railroad to run down the new track. The impasse was not resolved until September 1904, when the chancellor signed a decree permitting an elevated crossing at Newtown. The bridge was to be a span of 80 feet, approached by long trestles on each side. The estimated cost of construction was $20,000. By October 17, the bridge was finished and the first trolley crossed it.

While the dispute over the crossing of the railroad and the bridge building was in progress, JCT was extending the line through Keansburgh and Belford. They were also running traffic over the lines as the expansion progressed. Bricks were transported first by horse and wagon and then by trolley from the brickyard to build the new powerhouse. Mr. Samuel Haigh, the new superintendent of JCT, opened an office and waiting room on Front Street in October 1903 that was lighted by electricity. He also installed five electric lights at Freneau and Union (Beach) for the convenience of customers.

The first trip over the extension of the JCT line to Red Bank was made on April 1, 1904, on a flat car; the next day a number of citizens of Keyport, Red Bank, and Belford and officers of JCT made a formal trip to Red Bank and enjoyed a spread at Frick's Hotel. After speeches and several toasts, the party returned to Keyport in 45 minutes (including a walk across the railroad tracks at Union and change of cars). Regular scheduled service began on April 7. Three days later, the trolleys carried 2,259 passengers to and from Red Bank, some of them on the steps hanging on the outside. Fares were 5¢ from Freneau to St. Joseph's Church, 5¢ thence to Keansburgh, 5¢ thence to New Monmouth, and another 5¢ for the last leg to Red Bank.

JCT was also laying track northward and had reached the border of South Amboy, where there was some resistance. With one more mile of track in South Amboy and the bridge across the railroad at Union, the *Keyport Weekly* outlined the routes and connections to travel from Trenton to the Jersey Shore at a cost of about $1.50: via the Trenton & New Brunswick lines to Milltown Junction, from there to South Amboy via the Middlesex & Somerset division of Public Service, from South Amboy to Red Bank via the JCT, from Red Bank to Long Branch via Monmouth Traction Company, and at Long Branch, the cars would connect with the Atlantic Coast Electric Railway for Asbury Park, Ocean Grove, and Belmar.

Four new open trolleys arrived in July 1904. They ran almost noiselessly and were equipped with only 12 seats. Their arrival was celebrated with the Beach Park Band on board for the inaugural trip. In August, there were several washouts between New Monmouth and Red Bank that delayed traffic for several hours. Discussions started in Keyport to change the location of the tracks on Broadway from the East side of the street to the center. On Labor Day, JCT carried about 5,000 passengers. In front of the Old Homestead Hotel in Matawan in September 1904, a trolley struck Dud Bailey's wagon, throwing him out, and the frightened horse ran all the way to Keyport. The trolley was a fascinating new world, and sometimes the familiar old one could not quite cope with it.

With no fanfare on October 17, 1904, the first passenger trolley crossed the new bridge at Newtown with Inspector Elmer Hoffman acting as motorman. Thereafter, the trolleys left Keyport at 40 minutes after the hour for a through trip to Red Bank without change. Much greater notice was given to the discharge of Superintendent Samuel Haigh because the parent company in Philadelphia found it "manifestly impossible to tolerate friction in the management of this . . . business enterprise." He was replaced by Superintendent Bangs.

The *Keyport Weekly* noted in November 1904 that men crowded the rear platform of the trolleys to such an extent it was almost impossible for ladies and children to board the cars, even though there was usually ample room inside. Perhaps this was part of the reason for introducing new Brill semi-convertible cars. These cars could be converted for summer use by telescoping the windows into pockets in the roof. The company also took steps to provide more reliable

The new car barns and power house on Florence Avenue in Union (Beach).

power. They installed a powerful new backup generator for the power plant at Newtown and installed a new generator at the old power plant to provide power for electric lights.

Late in February, JCT lost a motorman in a tragic accident near Morgan. The last car for the night left South Amboy headed south with Everett Ward as the motorman. He started off at high speed and in the dark did not realize he had reached a sharp curve in the tracks. The car jumped the tracks and struck one of the electric light poles with such force that it demolished the pole. Everyone was thrown from the car, and Mr. Ward was found lying in a pool of blood with one leg severed. The passengers carried him to the car and applied a tourniquet. Two people walked in the dark for help, but by the time a doctor arrived, Mr. Ward had died.

Two modern conveniences were reported in April 1905. The clock in the waiting room of the JCT was set daily by Western Union time, and JCT installed a private telephone on a pole along the line in Browns Point for the convenience of employees to report an accident, delays, or other urgent business. A more significant item was reported that same month; JCT started soliciting business with a view of establishing day current. Up to that point, current was provided to customers outside the trolley lines in the evening hours when demands for the trolley were low. By July 1905, the *Weekly* was reporting that JCT had sold six more electric fans, and orders had also been filled for electric smoothing irons.

JCT was a pioneer in providing weather reports to the public. General Manager FD. Low arranged with the United States Weather Bureau in New York for weather predictions each evening and the day following; the report was posted

A JCT open car at the car barn.

in the trolley waiting room. This was prompted perhaps by an incident on July 10, 1905. One JCT car had just passed the Morgan Bridge when a thunderstorm erupted. Motorman Jesse Aumack stopped the car and ran to the rear to get his rubber boots. Before he could take the pole off the line a bolt of lightning hit between the car and the nearest lightning arrester, traveled back to the car, and burned out the controller with a loud explosion. The five passengers ran for a nearby cornfield instead of staying in the car. No one was hurt, but there were five wet and frightened passengers.

The trolleys were overflowing and extra cars were put into service for Memorial Day in 1905. Despite disagreeable weather in the morning, huge crowds thronged to Keyport to view the parade, the baseball games (Keyport lost a double header), and the entertainment at Pavilion Beach, where there was standing room only. The weather was better for the Fourth of July and crowds were huge again. In town, the excitement began at 1 a.m. with the ringing of the fire bell on town hall, which triggered the sounding of the triangle on Lincoln Hose. Actually, someone rang the bell on the school to celebrate the holiday and set a false alarm in motion. The trolleys ran extra cars, and packed every car like a sardine can all day long. An immense crowd visited Pavilion Beach even though admission had been raised to 25¢.

There was a tremendous explosion at the powerhouse in September 1906. Chief Engineer Frank Vanderbilt noticed that the large trolley engine being used to supply power did not sound right. He went over and started to shut the steam when the cast iron studs gave way and the whole top of the engine blew through the roof of the powerhouse. Although scalded by escaping steam, he managed to walk around the powerhouse and shut the steam at the boilers before passing out.

He was found, treated, and returned to duty not long after. The company made temporary repairs to the engine and decided to order a new one.

Regular traffic had been running between Keyport and Red Bank. However, the JCT lines ran only to Bridge Avenue in Red Bank, which left a gap of several blocks between it and the business section. In January of 1906, the Red Bank merchants petitioned the Board of Trade to have the JCT use the Long Branch trolley tracks so the JCT cars could run through to the business section. In March, the Red Bank Commissioners granted JCT a franchise to run to the "fountain" at the corner of Broad and Front Streets using the Long Branch trolley tracks on Monmouth Street. There were some minor delays, but after arrangements were made with the Monmouth Electric Company, this link was completed.

By April 1907, JCT had all the approvals necessary to build a link into Atlantic Highlands. It was to connect with the main line at Campbell's Crossing (Junction) and run along the County Road into Leonardville, across the meadows, and follow the railroad to Valley Drive. The franchise was granted by the Board of Freeholders on April 10. Work began immediately, and JCT requested and received permission to extend the trolley line down First Avenue and around the railroad station.

The *Keyport Weekly*, as early as November 1904, predicted that "as soon as the Jersey Central Traction Company's tracks are completed in South Amboy, there will be through service from Spring Lake to Jersey City." Little did they know that this dream would take years rather than months to accomplish. In May of 1905, JCT and the Public Service Corporation had about 100 men working on finishing the link between the two lines at South Amboy. The last rails were laid on May

The Morgan draw bridge brought the Jersey Central Traction lines almost to South Amboy.

10, but by July the JCT cars were still denied access to South Amboy. It wasn't until March 1906 that the South Amboy Borough Council granted JCT a franchise to run to the Central Railroad station. To accomplish this, JCT had to pay the collector $50, the Borough Counsel $100, and pave Broadway with macadam from Henry to John Street. By December, JCT had awarded a contract with Beers Brothers to grade the roadbed from South Amboy through Sayreville. In July 1907, JCT received franchises to build its lines to and across the Raritan River Bridge. In return for the bridge franchise, JCT agreed to build its own trestle next to the county bridge, light the bridge, and furnish power to turn the draw.

In November 1907, Public Service Corporation brought certiorari proceedings against JCT for its bridge franchise. The judge, however, allowed JCT to proceed with the work pending further hearings. In May 1908, JCT and Public Service Corporation worked out an agreement to let the companies use each other's tracks. This enabled Public Service to reach the shore resorts and JCT to reach Perth Amboy and Rahway. At about this time, JCT issued a map for its customers showing the territory covered as well as proposed extensions. Included was a link between Freneau [Matawan] and Freehold.

JCT had to ask for an extension of time for the bridge project in June 1909 because there were problems obtaining a right of way on the South Amboy side to reach the bridge. At a hearing before the Perth Amboy Board of Trade, JCT satisfied the board that the hold-up was a disagreement with the Pennsylvania Railroad Company and had since been satisfactorily resolved. The Board granted a one-year extension.

In the meantime, JCT was faced with a dilemma. It had permission from South Amboy to run its line through the "hole in the wall" to get under the railroad. However, to do this, it would have to dig it deeper, which would jeopardize the structure and create a flooding problem. The railroad had offered an alternate route to run under its lines. On July 29. 1909, JCT requested approval for the other route, and on September 7 the new franchise was granted.

Work on the trolley trestle between South Amboy and Perth Amboy started on November 4 and was halted by the War Department two weeks later. There was concern the new structure would interfere with navigation by halting the flow of ice when it broke up for the winter. All objections were withdrawn on November 30. By April 1910, the river crossing was complete, and tracks were being laid through Perth Amboy. On August 2, there was a formal opening of traffic across the bridge and through Perth Amboy for connection with the Public Service Company lines. The prediction of service through to Jersey City made in 1904 was finally a reality, yet there were still a few minor bumps ahead. In April 1911, the JCT ran its cars from Smith Street in Perth Amboy to Woodbridge Creek over the Public Service Corporation tracks. The two companies were sharing lines, but there were bad feelings between the crews of the two companies. This erupted into a fight on the bridge between the Amboys when a car from each company met in the middle of the bridge. Shortly thereafter, two Public Service cars boxed in a JCT car on the run between Perth

The trolley trestle (or "S" bridge) over the railroad tracks in Union (Beach).

Amboy and Woodbridge Creek. The Public Service people were demanding the JCT use that section of track only when following one of their cars; this of course would mean little ridership for the JCT cars. After negotiation, JCT agreed not to sell bargain tickets in Perth Amboy.

There were to be two more extensions of trolley lines in the history of the JCT. In November 1911, the JCT proposed running a line from the fountain in Red Bank to Long Branch and down Broadway to the new pier at the Oceanfront. They amended it to call for a loop via Third Avenue to the train station. In July 1912, the Monmouth County Board of Freeholders granted the franchise, including permission to use the Gooseneck Point Bridge, to cross the Shrewsbury River. In return, the JCT agreed to furnish power to light the bridge and to pay one-third the cost of a new bridge if needed in 12 years. The final extension of JCT lines was from Palmer Avenue, Keansburg, via Carr Avenue, to the Steamboat Dock. In May 1914, the JCT increased its capital stock from $1.5 million to $5 million.

Traffic continued on the JCT lines except one day in January 1907 when trees knocked down the electric light and trolley lines, along with the telephone line at Walnut Street in Keyport. There was such a mix-up of wires that electricity from two powerhouses had to be shut down for an hour and a half. Facilities that year were expanded with additional offices next to the waiting room, a new 1,000-horsepower steam turbine, and a temporary paint shop on the Florence Avenue property while the car barns were being completed. This construction was delayed because the bridge across Matawan Creek had to be repaired and strengthened. Up until then, the company had been hauling the heavy loads of brick over that line.

The line ran beyond Atlantic Highlands to Highlands. This view (from a post card) is from August 1, 1907.

Frederick Bangs was succeeded by A.R. Dimick as superintendent in May 1907. Mr. Dimick had been superintendent of the Oregon Water Power and Railway Company in Portland, Oregon. Mr. Bangs was placed in charge of the Newtown Power House. One of Mr. Dimick's first actions was to announce a raise for conductors and motormen to 20¢ and 23¢ per hour. The raise was unexpected and well received.

Sometimes an accident on the trolleys was caused by a simple malfunction. In September 1907 on a Saturday night, the JCT ran trailers (one trolley behind another) to accommodate the large number of passengers. In coming around a curve, the pole of the first car slipped off the feed wire, stopping the trolley and leaving it in darkness. The second came along at a fast clip, did not see the first one, and crashed into it. Several people were injured.

A much more serious accident occurred in November at the car barns on Florence Avenue. James O'Toole was working alone there. He had run a car out of the barn and into the main line by opening a switch. When he pulled the car forward to return it to the barn, the trolley pole left the wire. He was behind the car trying to return the pole to the wire, when a trolley returning from Red Bank veered off the main line because of the open switch and headed toward the trolley Mr. O'Toole was working on. Despite all attempts to stop and to warn him, the two trolleys collided with Mr. O'Toole in between. He was instantly beyond human aid.

The life of a conductor or motorman could be dangerous. On a trip out of Red Bank, a conductor was trying to maneuver around a lady with a very large hat to collect a fare. Just when he thought he was safely around the hat, the lady turned her head. A hatpin that protruded several inches beyond the hat connected with the point of the conductor's nose, resulting in a crimson stream. He managed to staunch the flow, and completed his duties.

Horses were sometimes victims of the trolleys. Farmer James Hanoway was returning late by horse and wagon from Keyport to Union. He fell asleep and left the horse to find its way. The horse followed the trolley tracks and, in crossing the trestle near the powerhouse, fell through. After several hours' effort by a crew of men, the poor horse was extricated but had to be destroyed. In another instance, a farm hand was driving a loaded wagon drawn by two horses parallel to a trolley. The trolley signaled, but the farm hand suddenly cut right in front. In the collision, one horse was killed outright and the other had to be destroyed.

One motorman gained quite a reputation as an opossum catcher. They were to be found along the tracks at night, and the glare of the headlight would entrance them. The motorman caught many of them. Do you think he liked opossum pie?

Four large new cars were purchased by the JCT from the Brill Company in December 1910; with this addition, the company had 18 closed cars. The first of these was given the number 34 and placed on the Red Bank run in charge of Motorman William C. Wharton and conductor Michael Hourihan. These, at 43 feet in length, were some of the largest cars in New Jersey. They were equipped with four 50-horsepower motors, air brakes, electric heaters, and arc lights.

A series of improvements was ushered in in 1911 and 1912. In order to prepare for holding the Monmouth County Fair in Middletown, the JCT installed double tracks in the Minnisink Park area at the Fields farm. A.A. Churchill of Keyport designed a pile driver for mounting on a trolley bed that

Trolley Waiting Station on First Street near the steamboat docks.

would fold flat until needed; with all of the piles needed in trolley lines, it was a welcome innovation. In January 1912, cash registers were installed in trolleys to replace the paperwork of day sheets kept by conductors. In August 1912, the JCT moved its offices and waiting room from Front Street to a new brick building on First Street overlooking the steamboat docks. In October 1913, a waiting room was built on the corner of First and Walnut Streets on property donated by George E. Langan for the comfort of passengers from the Lockport section of Keyport.

In February 1912, Glover F. Perin of Chicago succeeded William Moran as superintendent of the JCT. Only seven months later, he was succeeded by A.H. Mann of Lansing, Michigan. Chester Walling was promoted from dispatcher to superintendent of transportation. The first problem faced by Mr. Mann was a substantial increase in assessment of Raritan Township properties. (Keyport at that time was still a part of Raritan Township.) Mr. Mann replaced George Walling, who was responsible for accounting, with Miss Axe from Mr. Mann's hometown of Lansing. Captain Stephen Stoney, who had been a motorman for the company longer than any other employee, was granted a leave of absence in November 1913 to try his hand at raising chickens. In this period, the *Keyport Weekly* gave the JCT a top rating for on-time service, comfort, and modern facilities despite the fact that there were complaints about the service to Red Bank. An example given was the trolley leaving Campbell's Junction on November 22; it was an old-style car with a seating capacity of 40, but it carried 127 passengers straight to Red Bank and left many others waiting for the next trolley. There was

Trolley station at Palmer Avenue in Keansburg.

also criticism of the service to Matawan Station. The Keyport cars for Matawan Station were at times delayed waiting for the arrival of the Red Bank cars and, as a result, missed the train connection.

Sometimes automobiles were dangerous near trolleys. In August of 1913, two JCT employees were injured by them. Louis Mount was collecting fares and standing on the trolley running board when a car hit him and sent him flying 25 feet; the car sped away without being identified. Joseph Rowan, conductor of the company's freight train, was standing by his train when a car struck him and then sped away without being identified.

In October 1913, a horse and carriage tangled with a trolley. Michael Murphy, a commission merchant, was driving home and approaching a trolley crossing where the view was obstructed by a building. He saw the trolley too late and tried to get across ahead of it. Both Mr. Murphy and his horse were struck and killed. In December, the trainmen asked for a raise of 2¢ per hour. Earlier, they had been provided with a clubroom at the trolley waiting station complete with billiard tables. As a result, the trainmen were reluctant to ask for a raise. The Public Service trainmen were given a raise, however, and it was expected that their request would be granted.

In January 1915, the JCT agreed to pay half the $40,000 cost to build a new drawbridge across Matawan Creek. The structure was designed to carry trolley as well as carriage traffic in both directions. It was designed as a lift draw (with the section to be opened 75 feet) and was built 150 feet south of the old span to minimize interruption during construction. In March 1915, the company was sold by the Morris brothers of Philadelphia to Laird & Company of Wilmington, Delaware. At about this time, the company introduced new modern cars for the Matawan-Keyport and Matawan-Freneau divisions; made of steel and the interiors finished in mahogany, the cars were equipped with all the latest features.

In June 1917, through a merger, the JCT agreed to sell its powerhouse, substations and lines to Monmouth Lighting Company. This was approved by the utility board along with the merger of Monmouth Lighting Company and the Middlesex & Monmouth Electric Light, Heat & Power Company. This served to separate the traction companies from the power companies and put the control of the generating plants and substations in the hands of the lighting company.

The country had entered the World War, and the United States Fuel Administration asked the electric railways to conserve coal by reducing the 16 million tons per year consumed by 1 million tons. The JCT responded by not heating its cars, but there were many complaints. The shortages of coal that developed also affected service, because fewer trolleys could be run.

JCT asked for a fare increase of 2¢ in April 1918 and was granted an increase of 1¢ per zone in September. The increase was requested because the roadbeds were in need of repair, an increase in wages had to be granted, and the cost for power had increased. In parallel, the company had requested that the fare be increased to 8¢. Under the existing rate of 6¢, the JCT showed the losses already sustained and estimated further losses to the end of the year of $23,000. In addition, it was necessary to improve the roadbed and purchase several cars to accommodate the vast army of government workers at the Morgan arsenal. The State Board of Public Utilities Commission instead granted a 1¢ increase, making the fare in each zone 7¢. The company was still losing money and hard pressed to provide all of the necessary service with the equipment available. It petitioned for an additional raise of 3¢ per zone, and there was little opposition at the hearings in April 1920.

In addition to the battles to increase fares, the JCT was faced with an increase in price for power in June 1920 and a trolley strike in July 1920. The company reported losses of $15,000 per month. One week after settling for a 5¢ per hour increase for the trainmen, the Public Utilities Commissioners rejected the request to raise fares from 7¢ to 10¢ per zone. They cited the need to make certain repairs first; a state inspector found the roadbed to be in deplorable condition. In its busiest season, JCT was faced with another problem. Monmouth Lighting Company had to make major repairs to the power plant. Furthermore, the state engineer's office required major repairs to the bridge across the Raritan River, which caused its closing for an extended period of time. For highway traffic, this meant a detour of about 25 miles; for the JCT, it meant terminating all traffic at the railroad station in South Amboy.

In 1917, the JCT showed a surplus in its books of $145,000; by 1920, it showed a deficit of $80,000. A considerable share of the operating cost of the company derived from franchises that had to be paid to the municipalities along its routes. In addition, the costs for supplies and labor had risen, while the fares had been held to a minimum. The cost of coal alone had risen from $1.90 per ton in 1917 to $7.50 per ton in 1921.

Measures were obviously necessary to recoup the losses. In April 1921, the JCT tried to abandon franchises that were not cost effective. The service from Freneau to the railroad tracks was not heavily traveled, and the tracks down Carr Avenue to the dock in Keansburg was seasonal, and Keansburg was demanding that the JCT resurface its roadbed. The JCT petitioned the Public Utilities Commission to abandon these services. The commission refused to allow abandonment of the Matawan service, and held over the decision regarding the Keansburg service. In the same petition, the JCT again asked for a fare raise to 10¢.

One-man cars were introduced on the Freneau-Matawan line in February and on the Keyport-Matawan line in March. The company made plans to run one-man cars on the entire line for the winter months. Existing cars could be used by closing the rear door and using the front door for entrance and exit; the reduction in labor was another attempt to reduce costs. There was some rejection by commuters at first, but within a couple of months the change was accepted.

The financial woes of the JCT continued, however. Much of the Keyport-Matawan roadbed had to be rebuilt, many bridges were in need of repair,

Trolley near Walnut Street in Keyport.

the bridge across the Raritan River had to be removed and the tracks rerouted across the new highway bridge, and tracks had to be removed in Perth Amboy. Many of these changes were required because several areas had come under county or state highway authorities.

At this time, there was great agitation to move the tracks running down Broadway in Keyport from the east side of the road to the center. Part of the concern, however, was the desire of residents to have the road paved. Hearings were held, the JCT explained that it could not afford such a change, and the Freeholders agreed to pave the road along the JCT roadbed. Everyone was satisfied, and demand to change the roadbed was withdrawn.

Finally in April 1922, the Public Utilities Commission granted the requested increase in fares to 10¢. However, as part of the package, the company was required to sell special commutation tickets for frequent users; in effect, this kept the 7¢ fare for frequent commuters and raised the fare for only the occasional rider.

By May 1922, there was a request before the Keyport Council for a franchise for jitney service, but the council refused to grant it. In the same month, General Manager Hitchcock stated, "Unless this rate [10¢] produces sufficient revenue to enable the Company to pay its obligations, it cannot continue to operate." The revenues were not sufficient, and in May 1923 the JCT applied to the Public Utilities Commission to abandon all of its lines and surrender its charter. In July, the commission granted the application, and all traffic ceased on July 28, 1923.

There were many applications to the Keyport Council following the demise of the JCT for franchises for bus service. Some of those applying were Ackerman

Brothers, Rollo Trucking, and Mr. Foosaner for the service between Keyport and Matawan; and James Doukas for the service to the Amboys. On July 29, Rollo Trucking Corporation started service on the Keyport-Matawan-Freneau route, Marathon Bus Company (James Doukas) started service to the Amboys, and the Shore Bus Line started picking up passengers for Keansburg on its way from Newark. Later, the Triangle Bus Company was granted the franchise to provide service to Red Bank.

A very different sort of service was proposed by Herman Schlichting and Harry P. Robinson of Red Bank in October of 1923. They purchased the JCT tracks between Red Bank and Keyport and proposed to run gasoline-driven cars over the tracks. However, they were not successful in putting the line into operation.

Trolley running through Keyport's business section.

10. Those Flying Machines: Aeromarine and Burnelli

February 1917 opened one of the most interesting chapters in Keyport history. The Aeromarine Plane & Motor Company came to town and ushered in a whole new way of life. Up until then, airplanes and flying were notions people talked about, but few had actually seen. The Wright brothers had flown in 1903 down south in North Carolina. Peter and Thomas Walling of Tinton Falls had built an airplane and flown it in 1910, but it crashed. All that had been seen in the skies over Keyport were birds.

Joseph Boland, with his brothers Frank and James, designed and built a plane and had successfully flown it in 1909 over nearby Iselin; Frank created the airframe and Joseph designed the engine. In that year, Joseph and Frank Boland founded the Boland Airplane & Motor Company in Newark. In 1911, Ella Uppercu became a partner, and in 1913, Frank Boland's widow sold the rest of her interest to Inglis Uppercu, husband of Ella Uppercu. The company was re-incorporated that year as the Aeromarine Plane & Motor Company. Even with new facilities opened in Newark and Nutley, there was not enough space for mass manufacturing.

In April 1916, Aeromarine purchased what was formerly the Robbins Brickyard tract in Keyport, 60 acres on the bay with a three-story brick building. The facilities were extended to several buildings, a landing strip, and a railroad siding to serve the new plant. Aeromarine came to Keyport with a contract for 200 training planes for the Navy, valued at $2 million with over 100 employees.

Among those in the original group were: Joseph Boland, Joseph Morley, Ed Riley, James Delaney, George Ayers, Richard Greisinger, George Fritz, Elmer Straub, Harry Martin, Kenneth Stone, Ed Musick, Paul and Cy Zimmerman, and Paul Ash. Many people from Keyport and the surrounding areas were added to the roles in order to keep the production line going. By June of 1917, the company had grown to 1,200 employees under General Manager Hugh Robinson, who had earlier been associated with Glenn Curtiss. Robinson promoted Paul G. Zimmerman to Chief Engineer.

Assembly line for training planes at the Aeromarine plant.

In 1917, the sight of airplanes in the sky went from something never seen before to commonplace. Furthermore, this tranquil town was rocked by the constant roar of engines being tested. The grounds were surrounded by fences patrolled by guards, because there were always fears of German spies not only in Keyport but also throughout the country. The plant was a beehive of activity and yet deliveries were slow in coming. There was even an official inquiry and severe criticism. At Aeromarine, constant improvements were being made during production. This took time, so deliveries were delayed.

Deliveries were made in full, however. The original intention of the company was to ship planes to their destination in Bay Shore, Long Island, but they were flown there instead. The first of these flights took place on August 10, 1917, with two Navy lieutenants at the helm. The flight took 40 minutes.

When the war ended in November 1918, Aeromarine had perhaps the finest facility for producing aircraft in the country, but no more demand for them from the government. There were 16 fireproof buildings comprising 130,000 square feet. The facilities included a materials-testing laboratory, a wood shop, a hull shop, a plating department, a machine shop, a propeller department, a final assembly room, a welding department, a motor department, and a testing laboratory. All facilities had the latest equipment. Inglis Uppercu pursued every possible avenue to utilize the full potential of this well-equipped factory. In the winter of 1918–1919, he converted several of the military training planes for civilian use. Then in the summer of 1919, Aeromarine was awarded a contract for modifying 75 observation planes for the Army Air Service. Inglis Uppercu testified before a congressional committee in December 1919 that:

> We have tried in every way to turn our airplane plant into other purposes to help keep the airplane division in the plant, but I must confess that we are losing a large sum of money every week, and that will run into several hundred thousand dollars this year.

Three gentlemen from Havana conceived the idea of an air service between Cuba's capital and Key West, Florida, and they founded the Compania Cubana Americana de Aviacion. They ordered three Aeromarine flying boats for use in this service. Aeromarine Plane & Motor Company put the aircraft into production and prepared to ship them. Pilot Cy Zimmerman was put in charge of re-assembling and checking out at Key West. He suggested instead that he fly one of them down. With some trepidation, the company approved his proposal. On October 27, 1919, he and his mechanic, Richard Greisinger, set out on a flight to Key West and then Havana. When they landed in Key West, Cy Zimmerman found the other planes that had been shipped by train and supervised the assembly as well as some minor refurbishing of the plane he had flown. He and two other pilots then flew the planes to Havana for delivery to the Cuban company. After a warm welcome in Havana, they set out on a return flight to Keyport. In his log, Cy Zimmerman states:

> "November 16—Went down to the Custom House and looked over the three boats all of which were riding nicely at their moorings with their Cuban flags on one wing and American on the other, and my boat with

View over the rooftops showing the huge facility for producing aircraft.

> Mr. Uppercu's flag below the Cuban, and Columbia Yacht Club below the American. All three boats were remarkably clean and free from oil and a sight to be proud of, riding at their moorings with El Morro Castle as a background."

The Aeromarine Log then goes on to tell of a return flight to Keyport. The trips down and back were accomplished with several stops, but as stated in the log, the 3,062 miles were covered in 50 hours, 9 minutes flying time. The Cuban company, because of financial problems, operated only sporadically, mainly in Cuba, before disappearing from the scene.

The Navy had a very large stockpile of flying boats from various manufacturers. They were crated and being held in warehouses, and with the war over, it did not appear that these planes would ever be put to use. It should be remembered as well that all planes in those days were wood-frame with a doped fabric cover. Deterioration of these crates was just a matter of time.

Inglis Uppercu saw the commercial possibilities in the Curtiss flying boats and proposed that the Navy sell a quantity of them to him for conversion to commercial use. Rear Admiral Moffett, chief of the Navy's Bureau of Aeronautics, endorsed this proposal as a responsible method of conversion to civilian use. Aeromarine purchased several of the large F-5Ls as well as several of the three or four-seater HSs with an enclosed cockpit cabin cover. The first modified F-5L was completed in the early summer of 1920 and described as America's premier commercial airliner. The forward cabin contained six large wicker armchairs, upholstered in brown leather, three on each side of a central aisle. Each seat had a window 18 inches in diameter, which could be opened in flight if the passenger so desired. A rear cabin had five seats and a divan. The soundproof interior was lined with mahogany veneer. There were carpets and drapes, dome lights for night flying, cigar lighters, and vanities. Accommodations for the three-man crew were functional. The cockpits were open but provided excellent visibility. Two 400-horsepower Liberty engines provided a speed of 75 miles per hour and an endurance of six hours. Six more F-5Ls were completed along with several of the smaller craft.

As a first step in marketing commercial flight, Inglis Uppercu formed the Aeromarine Sightseeing and Navigation Company. With the F-5L, he carried more than 1,000 passengers between New York and the resorts of Atlantic City, Southampton, and Newport. This first experiment was so successful that he made plans for establishing regular scheduled airlines, something that had not been done in this country. A company (Florida–West Indies Airways) had been formed by others to provide mail service between Key West and Havana, and they had secured the first airmail contract in American history (F.M.-1). However, they did not have the capital needed to establish the service. Their stock was offered to the public but remained unsold until Inglis Uppercu made an offer. In October 1920, a merger took place with Uppercu holding the controlling interest and a change of name to Aeromarine West Indies Airways.

That same month on October 23, the *Santa Maria* and the *Pinta*, which were both converted F-5Ls, flew from New York to Key West, thus regular passenger and air mail service began to Havana on November 1 with twice-daily flights. When it became evident that the demand for passenger service was seasonal, Aeromarine dropped the mail contract in May 1921.

A summer-long promotional tour followed, which took the *Santa Maria* on a 7,000-mile journey to New York, Toronto, Buffalo, Detroit, Chicago, New Orleans, and a return to Key West. Another promotional tour, using a remodeled HS-2L, left New York on July 7. The six-passenger flying boat stopped at cities bordering Lakes George, Champlain, Ontario, Erie, Huron, and Michigan. More than 500 passengers were carried on this 7,490-mile circumnavigation, and 100 landings were made. There were no air incidents on either of these extensive promotional tours.

The 1921–1922 season was very successful, but the crash of a plane of a rival airline that had started up served to dampen the public's enthusiasm. Aeromarine, although it had flown without incident, lost business. To a congressional committee, Charles F. Redden of Aeromarine said that, "When a mishap occurs, all aviation gets the blame." He went on to recommend that the federal government take on responsibility for inspecting aircraft and licensing pilots. A bill to accomplish this was proposed in Congress but failed to pass. Again, Aeromarine had asked the federal government to enter the field of commercial aviation by providing needed regulation.

Zimmerman and Greisinger, who made the first flight to Havana via Key West.

By the summer of 1922, Aeromarine Airways was operating two divisions, Eastern and Great Lakes. Daily service between Cleveland and Detroit was started on July 17 and a second flight was added shortly thereafter. During the two months this route operated, Aeromarine carried 4,388 passengers. In the fall of 1922, Aeromarine Airways secured a new contract for the Key West–Havana route. There were plans to expand operations throughout the West Indies, and Charles Redden predicted that the time was not far distant when the general public would accept air travel as a desirable and necessary means of transportation. This optimism was dashed in January 1923 when the flying boat *Columbus* developed engine trouble, landed in heavy seas, and sank. Four passengers were lost and a passing steamer rescued everyone else. This time, the disaster had struck Aeromarine. Following this, one of the flying boats, at anchor in Havana harbor, was destroyed in a storm.

Coupled with these disasters, the effects of high overhead could no longer be ignored. For every $100 spent, 69 percent went to insurance, depreciation, and sales promotion. On the other hand, for true operating costs, only 15 percent went to fuel and labor and 16 percent to maintenance. The insurance was prohibitive in large part because of the lack of federal regulation. The labor cost was only $90 per week for Aeromarine pilots and $55 per week for mechanics.

Hull of Model 50 B-2 flying boat. For the year 1920, the design was far ahead of its time.

The effects of air disasters and crushing overhead costs caused the otherwise very successful Aeromarine Airways to fade from the picture around 1923. There were no federal subsidies to promote commercial aviation as there were in several foreign countries. During these years of providing the inaugural scheduled commercial air service in the country, Aeromarine was responsible for several firsts. They provided the first meals served in flight, the first stewards, the first movies shown in flight, the first use of radio in commercial flight, and the first baggage stickers for luggage carried in flight.

From 1920 to 1923, Aeromarine brought in a different kind of employee. Harry Bruno was brought in to sell commercial flight on Aeromarine planes to the public. In this capacity, he was probably the first of the public relations men. His official title was sales and advertising manager, and he was given a luxurious office in the Times Building in Manhattan. As he says in his book *Wings Over America*, he seldom got to see the Times Building except from the cabin or cockpit of an Aeromarine flying boat.

Harry Bruno was constantly on the move at first with flights into New England cities with a river, harbor, or lake where he could land one of their flying boats. All manner of local officials and businessmen were treated to flights and Harry Bruno, his pilot, and mechanic were in turn hosted at dinners in their honor. There would be banner headlines in the local papers announcing their arrival. In their wake, they left people who were building landing sites for sea or land planes. From the planes, Harry took aerial photos. His photos of Manhattan were that city's first aerial views, and were featured in the Sunday rotogravure supplements.

Aeromarine ran special flights to Atlantic City, charging a high price but serving an increasing clientele. Bruno addressed and recruited sportsmen to sell the idea of flight and a few planes were sold. For William Wrigley, thousands of sticks of gum were dropped over several cities. The flight that circumnavigated the Great Lakes has been mentioned previously. Bruno used this too as a vehicle for publicizing commercial flight.

Harry Bruno still found that many people were afraid of this new transportation. He tried flying infants, publicized the pet dogs of the pilots, and finally tried glamour. Many flights and photographs for the media showed Broadway showgirls enjoying trips on Aeromarine Airways. The first airline baggage sticker was the creation of Harry Bruno. The publicity stunt to transport a Ford car from Detroit to Cleveland was a Bruno creation and the first case of flying an automobile from one place to another. Despite all of Harry Bruno's efforts, however, Aeromarine Airways failed because of economics, and he went on to other companies and other challenges after only three years with the company.

While these activities were in progress with Aeromarine Airways, several things were happening back at the plant. They designed and built the model 50 B-2 three-passenger flying boat, which was exhibited at the Chicago Air Show in January 1920. The cabin for passengers was in front of the wings with the pilot sitting behind. The roof of the cabin was made of celluloid sheets

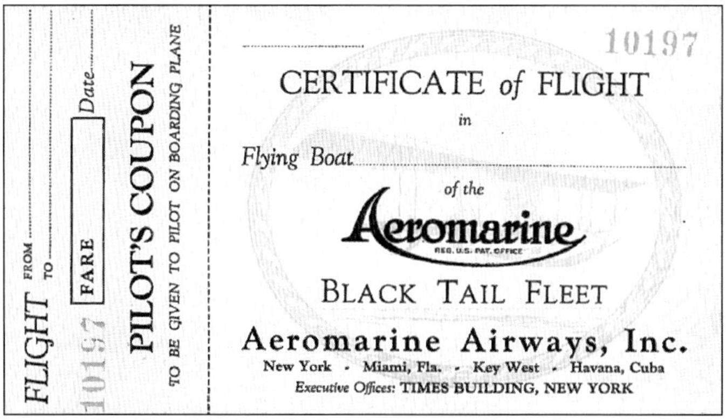
FLIGHT FROM TO
10197
FARE
Date
PILOT'S COUPON
TO BE GIVEN TO PILOT ON BOARDING PLANE

10197
CERTIFICATE *of* FLIGHT
in
Flying Boat
of the
Aeromarine
REG. U.S. PAT. OFFICE
BLACK TAIL FLEET
Aeromarine Airways, Inc.
New York · Miami, Fla. · Key West · Havana, Cuba
Executive Offices: TIMES BUILDING, NEW YORK

Flight ticket for Aeromarine Airways.

set in a strong frame. The interior of the cabin was blue leather with polished mahogany trimmings, and the seats had spring backs. The plane was powered with an Aeromarine 130-horsepower, 8-cylinder, V-type engine. It was 29 feet long, 12 feet high, and would carry a useful load of 820 pounds at a speed of 75 miles per hour. This was the same plane flown to Havana for delivery to the Cuban company.

As a result of the Air Show, a deal was consummated with Harry Newman of Continental Aircraft, Inc., for distribution of all Aeromarine production west of the Alleghenies. The estimated value of the deal was $2 million. However, it does not appear this agreement resulted in any major flow of real dollars to Aeromarine.

In parallel with development of the Model 50 B-2, Aeromarine developed for the Navy a special light seaplane for scouting with the fleet at sea. It was powered with a Wright-Hispano engine and designed to lift off from the sea within 5 seconds.

In April 1921, a branch of Aeromarine Plane and Motor Company was consumed by flames. The New Jersey Motor Sales Company was in the building that had been the car barn for the Keyport & Matawan Street Car Company and was located on Broadway near the present-day Highway 35 overpass. The plant manufactured Ford marine engines for use in speedboats manufactured by Aeromarine Company. The fire resulted in a loss of approximately $60,000 and the company's insurance was inadequate.

In 1923, the company entered the competition for supplying a plane for cross-country mail service. The plane designed for this service had a metal fuselage. There had been experiments since 1922 on use of a sheet-aluminum alloy for this purpose. The government delayed appropriating funds for the mail planes, however, and there were long delays. In 1925, Aeromarine sold a flying boat with an all-metal hull made from sheets of 17S alloy, which is more commonly referred to as duralumin. The flying boat was a biplane designed for commercial passenger traffic. Its capacity was seven passengers with a crew of two. Named *Miss Key Largo City*, it was flown to Miami for delivery to the Fairchild Flying Company and for service between Miami and Key Largo City.

Joseph Boland, who with his brother had started the original company that became Aeromarine, continued as an engine designer. In 1926, his creation of an inertia starter for engines generated considerable interest within the industry. The company signed a contract to furnish a quantity of the starters to the Navy and at the same time one for propellers for the Army. The inertia starter built up tremendous energy in a compact unit housing a flywheel. In a fraction of a minute, sufficient power was released to start a 600-horsepower engine, all of this from a unit weighing 5 pounds and only 5 inches in diameter.

Joseph Boland's talent for invention started early. As a young boy, he gathered a quantity of spools, rigged them up around the house with connecting cords, and proceeded to put this crude power transmission system to work. He arranged to drop a saucepan on top of the family cat sleeping in the kitchen by pulling a cord in the parlor. His mother did not approve of this first invention, but his inquiring mind never stopped developing other contrivances. He did not like school and quit to enter the working world, where he went into the bicycle and farm machinery business, and ended up inventing a motorcycle. He went from job to job before he was hired as an automobile designer and draftsman with the Canada Manufacturing Company of Carteret in 1910 and then with the Automatic Air Carriage Company. With this background, he and his brother Frank formed their own aircraft company, as described above.

By 1929, Boland had invented a radial air-cooled engine for aircraft. The nine fixed cylinders developed 115 horsepower and revolutions per minute of over 1,900. In the severe tests for the Bureau of Standards, the engine had to undergo a test of 25 hours continuous running and maintain revolutions per minute of at

Airways Model 75 flying boat anchored by Aeromarine plant.

least 1,875. The engine exceeded all requirements. In 1931, Boland was granted three more patents: one for a valve mechanism, one for valve gears, and one for bearings. Another patent was granted in 1932 for an engine lubricating system. In 1931, Aeromarine started production of 100 of the AR-3 engines developed by Joseph Boland. The AR-3 was extremely light in weight and developed 50 horsepower at 2,125 revolutions per minute. It was designed for use in one- and two-passenger light planes.

When the Aeromarine plant closed, Joseph Boland formed a partnership with Mitzie Strang under the name Mitzie's Battery and Machine Shops. They operated two automobile and airplane repair shops in the Matawan area. Even after his work with Aeromarine ended, Joseph Boland continued with his inventions. In 1934, he was granted a patent for a vibration dampener for aircraft engines.

Inglis Uppercu was born on September 17, 1877, in Evanston, Illinois, son of Jesse Wheat and Laura Uppercu. He graduated from Brooklyn Polytechnic Institute and then, largely because his father was a lawyer, he attended Columbia University Law School. His interest in things mechanical prevailed, however, and in 1896 he became a mechanic for the Duryea Automobile Company in Carteret. Later he was associated with making the Gasmobile car. In 1902, he formed and headed up the Motor Car Company of New Jersey with sales rooms in Newark. In 1908, he bought the Cadillac Sales business in New York and formed the Detroit Cadillac Motor Car Company, which later became the Uppercu Cadillac Corp.

Early in life, Uppercu was very successful as a race car driver in the Vanderbilt Cup Races. He held patents for automobile devices he invented, and he became

Post card advertising Aeromarine West Indies Airways.

a pilot. Over the years, he acquired several mining interests in North Dakota, Montana, and Mexico; his holdings included gold, silver, and manganese deposits. He was an avid yachtsman and reconditioned and sailed a full-rigged clipper ship named the *Seven Seas*, which had been a Swedish naval training vessel.

Uppercu's main claim to fame, however, was his formation of Aeromarine Plane & Motor Company and its numerous subsidiaries. His leadership in the development and use of early aviation was virtually without parallel. He retired from the last of his business ventures, in the area of mining, in 1938. After a prolonged illness, he died in 1944 at his home in New York City.

In February 1926, the Aeromarine Plane and Motor Company consolidated with bus manufacturer Healey & Company. The Healey bus was designed with a direct front-wheel drive, a revolutionary concept for the time. With several orders in progress, expansion of the plant was projected. On top of this, negotiations were pending for the lease of space to Bellanca to produce their commercial plane at Aeromarine. Chamberlin had used this plane, designed by Guisseppe M. Bellanca, for his flight across the Atlantic. Bellanca also planned to establish regular air service between the United States and Europe. One model of the Bellanca plane had been assembled and tested. The plane was slated for a flight to Paris and was reputed to be the fastest in the country. On top of all this, the plane was able to carry 40 passengers—a lot for those days. At the last moment, the plane was seized via a writ of attachment for $1,400. There was no other attempt to produce Bellanca planes in Keyport.

In June 1928, Aeromarine announced that it would produce the German Klemm-Daimler monoplane at the factory in Keyport. Inglis Uppercu, president of Aeromarine, said that a new company had been formed for this purpose, the Aeromarine-Klemm Company. The planes were to be made in lots of 1,000 and were to sell for under $3,000 each. The Aeromarine-Klemm Company obtained the manufacturing rights in the United States for the German flivver plane, which had originally been developed for use as a glider. It was described as a "necessity development" for Germany because of the restrictions in place by the Treaty of Versailles. The 20-horsepower engine on the plane enabled it to fly 40 miles on a gallon of gas. In a test, it flew 1,800 miles in 32 hours. This was an exciting new step by Aeromarine to sell aviation to the public and capture a share in the market.

In December 1928, the new Klemm plane was exhibited at the International Aeronautical Exposition at Chicago. The first one sold at the show was to the Pegasians, a flying club in New York. Manufacture was slated to start in January 1929 at the rate of one plane per day in the beginning. The only part not manufactured at the plant would be the engine. In place of the 20-horsepower German version, the company substituted a 40-horsepower engine manufactured by Salmson and imported from France. Other minor changes made the Aeromarine-Klemm a heavier, stronger plane. An interesting feature also was that the wings could be reversed and attached to the side of the fuselage for transportation over highways. By the time of the exposition, the price had increased to between $3,500 and $4,000 per plane.

Stockholders of the new company voted on December 8, 1928, to purchase the land, consisting of 230 acres and buildings of the Aeromarine Plane and Motor Company. It was estimated that between 1,000 and 1,200 employees would be needed to produce the new plane.

In February 1929, two Klemms were on exhibit at the New York Aviation Show in Grand Central Palace. The two models of the Klemm produced were the *Mohawk* and the *Pinto*, one of which had tandem and the other side-by-side controls.

The Salmson engines were too expensive, and Aeromarine-Klemm soon switched to a 65-horsepower, five-cylinder LeBlond radial engine. Many of these popular light planes were sold. One famous buyer was Charles Lindbergh, who posed with millionaire Daniel Guggenheim in the cockpits of the plane. The timing of the introduction of the Klemm was too close to the stock market crash of 1929, however, and Aeromarine-Klemm closed its doors in 1931.

It was announced to the world in December 1928 that an entirely new, gigantic airplane had been built in secret at the Aeromarine plant in Keyport. The plane was all metal, using duralum, had retracting landing wheels, and incorporated two engines in the nose of the fuselage. Each had enclosed engine rooms with gas, oil, and water lines. This feature made it possible to get at the engines during flight without exposure. The plane was designed to carry a full load in flight on one engine. The wheels folded under glass domes so that they could be seen, and red lights indicated to the pilot when they were up. The cabin was luxurious, measuring 17 feet long by 11 feet wide, and finished in walnut. Seating comprised of swivel, overstuffed chairs. There were electric lights, cigar lighters, speed indicators for passengers to see, and behind were a kitchen, baggage room, wash room, and toilet. A searchlight mounted below the fuselage could be directed as needed including straight ahead for landing. The plane was designed to carry 20 passengers. The wing span was first reported as 89 feet and later as 91 feet. This first model was shipped off to Newark for test flights. Locally, this plane was referred to as the Flying Wing, because body and wing were so well blended that it appeared to be one giant wing in flight. Furthermore, the body or fuselage was designed to be an airfoil, which vastly improved the lift of the aircraft.

This first plane crashed during test flights when only 20 feet from the ground. Neither the pilot nor the mechanic was injured, and the pilot said that had there been passengers, they would not have been injured because the cushions had not even been shaken from the seats. The plane had been scheduled to make a mail pickup from the *Leviathan* at sea, but the demonstration had to be postponed.

Uppercu-Burnelli Corporation entered into an agreement with Societa Trans-Adriatica of Italy under which the Italian company would manufacture 50 planes per year for five years. The Italian Air Commission that negotiated the agreement was headed by General Balbo, who was famous for his transatlantic flight in 1933. During that flight, one of the Balbo planes developed mechanical problems and stopped at the Aeromarine plant for repairs.

The Burnelli plane was the largest ship on display at the New York air show in February 1930. One new feature of the design was that the metal skin on

The Burnelli transport with 32 people lined up to show the size of the plane.

the wings was smooth rather than corrugated. The company announced after the show that a number of the planes would be built at the plant in Keyport. A number of successful demonstration flights were conducted at Roosevelt field in July 1930. The interiors were decorated with green silk damask and the exteriors were green and orange.

The stock market crashed in 1929, however, and none of the Aeromarine ventures had been showing large returns. With the Aeromarine-Klemm Company out of business, the machinery was in receivership. In July 1931, Assessor George C. Smith had assessed the machinery at $92,000; on appeal, the assessor was directed to examine the machinery more closely. In February 1932, Inglis Uppercu bought the Aeromarine Klemm Corporation assets for $200,000. The assets included all real estate, buildings, machinery, products, supplies, accounts, and records but were subject to any other indebtedness including real estate taxes, which alone amounted to $42,000. Inglis Uppercu gambled on the success of the giant new plane. There were many potential applications for it including its use as a bomber for the military.

In March of 1932, it was announced that a large plane covered with gold leaf had been flown into Aeromarine field and rolled into a waiting hangar in an aura of great secrecy. No one, except one mechanic who could not speak English, was allowed any access to the plane. The announcement went on to say that the plane would be named the "Golden Eagle" and would be flown across the Atlantic by Lou Reichers. It was expected that the plane would set a world record, cutting in half the time taken by Charles Lindbergh. Alterations at Aeromarine would include installation of auxiliary gasoline tanks required for the long flight. The plane was owned by Bernard MacFadden, who was backing the flight.

Actress Ethel Barrymore posing by Aeromarine plane.

In January 1934, Inglis Uppercu appeared before the Keyport mayor and council to propose establishment of an airport in town. He offered to lease the Aeromarine field to the borough for $1 per year for 5 years. In return, he offered to assist the borough in applying for a Civil Works Administration grant to grade and complete the field. The proposition met with general approval, a committee was formed, and preparation of a lease went forward. Inglis Uppercu held discussions with officials in Washington to further the acceptance of an application from Keyport. Lou Reichers, in an interview with the papers on the subject, presented a prospect of an airfield stretching from the current Aeromarine field across the adjacent meadows of Conaskonk Point. He saw it as rivaling Newark Airport without the smoke and stacks of Newark industry. In the adjacent Raritan Bay he saw an ideal landing facility for seaplanes and flying boats. (Overseas air traffic then and extending into the beginning years of World War II was virtually all by flying boat.) When the lease prepared by Keyport was presented to Inglis Uppercu, however, he returned it unsigned. The borough had included a clause giving it the right to cancel the lease at any time during the five-year period, which was unacceptable to Mr. Uppercu. If Keyport had not exercised such extreme caution, there is a strong likelihood that one of the major New York area airports would have been located in Keyport.

Since the closing of Aeromarine Klemm Corporation in 1931, there had been very little activity at Aeromarine. Inglis Uppercu owned the plant, and

Vincent Burnelli had developed a gigantic new plane that held tremendous potential, but there was not enough working capital. Inglis Uppercu went to Washington to try to convince the Army or Navy to appropriate funds to produce a first model of a bombing plane developed by Aeromarine. The request was for a half million dollars for a model that would have four engines, fly 3,000 miles, and carry a load of 2,400 pounds at a much higher speed than any existing plane. For the day, these demands were for a plane way ahead of its time. The bomber plane was, of course, based on the huge plane developed by Vincent Burnelli. Federal funds would place Aeromarine back in operation and employ about 200 men, all of whom were readily available in the area—former Aeromarine employees.

While Inglis Uppercu was in Washington, Lou Reichers and Harry Boyce of Aeromarine addressed Raritan Post Number 23 of the American Legion to enlist support in the effort to make Aeromarine a thriving Keyport employer again. The Legion Post heartily endorsed the effort and proceeded to contact Senators Barbour and Kean and Congressman Sutphin, who all pledged assistance. Congressman Sutphin appeared before the Board of Review of the Reconstruction Finance Corporation (RFC) to urge that the government corporation grant a loan to Burnelli Aircraft Limited. The RFC was a federal government corporation established in 1932 to provide emergency financing facilities to aid in financing agriculture, commerce, and industry. Congressman Sutphin told them there were currently 60 men employed at the Keyport plant but that the loan would increase the number significantly. With the ongoing Depression, increasing employment was an extremely important matter.

In January 1935, the UB14, a Keyport-built Burnelli airplane, completed a successful test flight to Newark Airport, where it was scheduled to undergo a series of test flights for the Department of Commerce. This was part of the negotiation with the federal government for an RFC loan; meanwhile, discussions continued with the War Department regarding a proposed bomber plane. The RFC loan hinged on partial cancellation of tax liens on Aeromarine real estate holdings.

The UB-14 at Newark Airport had a fuselage (body) of an airfoil design to provide additional lift, which in essence made the plane a flying wing. From propeller to tail, it measured 40 feet and had a wingspread of 72 feet. There were two Pratt & Whitney engines of 875 horsepower each. The plane had comfortable cabins, baggage compartments, and a lavatory. The pilots sat in an enclosure on the leading edge of the wing. It would travel at up to 231 miles per hour and carried 400 gallons of gasoline. A week after arrival at Newark, the plane crashed. The co-pilot was hospitalized, but Lou Reichers, who was piloting the plane, was unhurt. The ailerons came loose, which caused a fluttering and loss of any ability to brake. The co-pilot had moved to the cabin when the fluttering started and so was not belted in place for the crash. The co-pilot recovered, but the plane was beyond repair.

Plans were announced later in the month for an advertising stunt using the older model of the Burnelli aircraft that had been built in 1930 and had been in storage for most of the time since. The project was arranged to bring in some capital and, at the same time, show that Burnelli aircraft were reliable. The project called for strapping a Ford car under the fuselage, flying to 10,000 feet and sub-zero temperatures, and then having an automobile race car driver climb down into the car and start it using Blue Sunoco gasoline.

With much fanfare, including an interview by Lowell Thomas, the event took place in February 1935. For Zeke Meyer, the racecar driver, this was his first flight in an airplane. When the plane was 1 mile high (not the 10,000 feet previously specified), Zeke Meyer opened a trap door in the bottom of the cabin and stepped down into the driver's seat. He was wearing a parachute and had been instructed on how to use it. The temperature was zero and the plane was travelling 130 miles per hour; the windshield of the Ford roadster broke the breeze somewhat, but the wind was still like an Arctic tornado. He pushed the starter, a bright light flashed, and the motor started up. Zeke Meyer was happy to climb back into the plane's cabin, however, to complete the flight in warmth and comfort. This was the story in the newspapers, but Lou Reichers, who was the pilot, told it differently.

Since there was no intercom, information had to be conveyed using hand signals. When Reichers saw that the temperature was zero, he nodded for the engineer to have Meyer climb down and start the car. The engineer thought he wanted to know whether the car was still hanging there. Meyer had not even climbed into the car. When Reichers took off, the Sunoco publicists sent out their news releases, so all flight participants were persuaded to go along with the story. Then they took off to really run the test. Everything went well until, after starting the car, Reichers started his approach to land. The car caught fire, because Meyer started it with the dashboard throttle and climbed back into the plane in a hurry. The car ran full throttle with the manual radiator shutters closed and caught fire. They managed to extinguish the blaze and made a successful landing.

Clyde Pangborn, the famous trans-ocean flyer, placed an order for a UB14B plane that he planned to use for a round-the-world flight. He had been the co-pilot for Roscoe Turner when he gained fame in the London-Australia flying derby. The goal in the proposed flight was to shave time from the mark set by Wiley Post in his world flight. His plans were to leave San Diego in August and fly 13,000 miles around the globe without having the wheels touch the ground. At strategic places, he planned to re-fuel in flight and complete the flight in four and a half days. The gasoline tanks of 2,500-gallon capacity would take up most of the cabin room, which in a normal configuration would have been the passenger cabin.

While construction of the above plane was in progress, sketches and bids were being prepared for a new bombing plane for the Navy. In addition, development was in progress for a five-cylinder engine based on the successful Boland AR-3 engine. Following this development, there were plans for two larger engines in the same series.

Clyde Pangborn tested the plane built for him by Uppercu-Burnelli Corporation in a flight to Red Bank airport. He was thoroughly pleased with the performance and even attained a cruising speed of 30 miles per hour beyond the calculated cruising speed of 200 miles per hour. At a luncheon at Blodgett's Restaurant at Six Corners in Keyport, Burnelli and Pangborn discussed setting new records on the present transcontinental air routes flown by mail and transport planes. It was felt that the Burnelli design could become the plane of choice for commercial aviation.

The new plane was equipped with controllable pitch propellers. This feature increased power on take off and reduced engine drag at cruising speeds. In addition, the pilots had maximum visibility in flight with a sliding hatch above and windows in the floor of the pilot compartments.

In July 1935, the plane was flown to Roosevelt Field in Long Island, where its capabilities were demonstrated and everything was recorded by the press. Veteran airmen at the field were impressed by the innovations incorporated in its design. From there the plane was flown to Washington for further demonstration of its

The men of the Engineering Department of Aeromarine who made so many groundbreaking developments and designs possible. Photo courtesy of Dan Kusrow.

capabilities for Army and other government officials. Discussions were still in progress on the possibilities of production of bombers at Uppercu-Burnelli.

The UB-14B plane was the center of attention at Red Bank Airport for Air Navigation Week in October 1935. There was great interest in the UB-14B safety features in the Copeland Senate Aviation Committee meeting in Washington. A letter to them from Clyde Pangborn presented a glowing appraisal.

In September 1936, Harry R. Boyce, manager of the Keyport plant of Burnelli Aircraft, Limited, applied to the Bureau of Air Commerce for authorization for a trans-Atlantic flight for the UB-14B. The flight was scheduled to be made before October 15. From this point, events moved swiftly.

The flight did not take place on October 15, but in October it was reported that the plane had been impounded. It was learned that Monty G. Mason of Mason Aircraft Limited had executed a chattel mortgage to several parties. Clyde Pangborn issued a show cause why the plane should not be sold to satisfy Pangborn's investment in the craft.

In November 1936, Burnelli Aircraft, Limited, went into receivership. Florence F. Forgotson, a stockholder in the company, also asked that the UB-14B plane be kept within the jurisdiction of the court. Cecil B. Ackerson, responding for the company, stated that the plane was then in New York because it was unable to land in Keyport due to weather conditions. Miss Forgotson charged wasting of assets, alleging that Burnelli Aircraft had borrowed $30,000 from a Canadian concern against the obligations of a company that became defunct. This action had the effect of deferring indefinitely the planned flight by Clyde Pangborn.

In the meantime, Burnelli achieved some success in England. Mass production of the plane was planned at British factories at London and on the Clyde. Licensing agreements were concluded with the Scottish Engineering Company, Limited, of London and were in process with the Canadian Car and Foundry Company of Montreal. In June of 1937, the UB-14B plane was loaded aboard the SS *Aquitania* and shipped to England for demonstration flights there and in Czechoslovakia. Company spokesmen indicated that Burnelli had contracts to build several planes for the British government. In July of 1937, the Canadian Car & Foundry Company removed the machinery and equipment from the Keyport plant. There was some talk at the time about the possibilities of the plant re-opening, but this was the end of Uppercu-Burnelli operations in Keyport and the end of an era.

As an anticlimax, in August 1937, the borough of Keyport took action for receivership of the lands and buildings in Keyport held by the Burnelli interests.

As Aeromarine was playing out its final chapter, in July of 1935, there was an announcement of a new aviation enterprise. Truly Blodgett revealed that a new light plane had been built in the old Keough building on the southwest corner of Front and Church Streets. The builder was Fred A. Anderson and the designer Renato Contini. (Renato Contini was one of the designers of the UB-14 at Uppercu-Burnelli.) The plane was called a "Speed Bird" and had a 28-foot wing span and an 85-horsepower Le blond engine. The Speed Bird Corporation took its plane to Fairview Flying Field at Red Bank for testing. Then the test pilot,

Vincent J. Burnelli, the genius who almost revolutionized aviation.

Ensign Ray B. Norby, flew it to Roosevelt Field where the plane was subjected to severe testing for the Department of Commerce inspector. One novel feature of the plane was that the passenger sat next to the pilot instead of in a cockpit ahead of the pilot, which had been standard up to then. The company planned to make several flights to promote interest with the public. There was backing from several people in Rumson. A site was being sought for mass production somewhere in the area. Either a site for production was found elsewhere or the company was not successful in going into production, but there seems to be no further mention of the Speed Bird.

About two years later, with the Aeromarine operations in receivership, negotiations started to induce the Taylor Plane Company to move its operations to the Aeromarine site. The Taylor Cub manufacturers were located in Bradford, Pennsylvania. Alfred Bennett of Hightstown was the individual trying to induce the move. The company's plant in Bradford had burned to the ground, and a new site was needed. There were over 100 offers throughout the country for a new location. The company, however, was leaning toward a location in Lock Haven, Pennsylvania. Furthermore, the Aeromarine facilities were much larger than the company needed. Lock Haven also arranged to purchase a large tract adjoining the facility there under consideration for a lease back for a nominal fee. A concerted effort was mounted to persuade the company to move to Keyport but to no avail. The borough thus came close to becoming the home of the Piper Cub of the Taylor Aircraft Company.

Inglis Uppercu, Joseph Boland, and Harry Bruno have been mentioned in previous sections. There were a host of others whose efforts combined to make Aeromarine great. There are some of these who need to be singled out for this chapter.

Cy Zimmerman was one of the earlier Aeromarine pilots. On August 7, 1919, he dropped a mailbag to the deck of the SS *Adriatic* while it was steaming across the Atlantic. He also made the first trip between Puerto Rico and New York.

Edwin C. Musick was also one of the earlier Aeromarine pilots. He later became a pilot for Pan American Airlines, flying the giant clipper planes. His flight in 1935 to Honolulu in 17 hours and 45 minutes broke all records.

The mechanics were just as colorful as the pilots, and flew with them. Mitzi Strang told of a stunt that called for him to climb out on a wing of an Aeromarine biplane over an ocean liner in New York harbor and toss a dozen roses to

William Douglas, vice president of Aeromarine, invented the front wheel drive for automobiles. He built the first model at Healey & Company for William K. Vanderbilt.

Douglas Fairbanks and his bride, Mary Pickford. The roses missed their mark, but Fairbanks retrieved a second hidden bunch and the media was satisfied. There were many more adventures involving Mitzi Strang.

Richard Greisinger was the mechanic for the flight with Cy Zimmerman to drop the mail pouch to the SS *Adriatic*. He was also the mechanic on the historic first flight to Havana from New York. The mechanics were one-man crews for the flying boats.

Lou Reichers was a trans-Atlantic flyer who flew for Aeromarine in the 1930s. He was the pilot for the trip carrying a car, which was started in mid-flight using Blue Sunoco gasoline.

Before coming to Aeromarine-Burnelli, Clyde Pangborn had made a record-breaking flight form Japan to Washington state in 1931 and had won, with Roscoe Turner, third place in the race from London to Melbourne, Australia. He had been slated for a round-the-world flight with the Burnelli UB-20 just before World War II.

This chapter would not be complete without a cohesive section on Vincent J. Burnelli. It relies heavily on five articles in *Aeroplane Monthly* by Howard Levy and Richard Riding. Vincent J. Burnelli was born in Temple, Texas. His father operated a wholesale fruit market there. Two of his brothers became writers for Lowell Thomas. Vincent went to New York at the age of 14, where he received his education and entered the field of aviation. In 1915 in Maspeth, with his friend John Carisi, he designed and built his first plane. His second design was for a night fighter, which never saw action in World War I, but was sold to the New York Police Department to start the aerial police. In 1919, he went to Milwaukee to design a commercial airliner seating 26 persons for Lawson Airlines. He was not happy with this design, however, and described it as a "streetcar with wings."

It was at this time that he devised the concept of the lifting fuselage in which the body or fuselage is shaped to add to the lift of the plane rather than provide a dead weight to overcome. In 1920, he teamed up with T.T. Remington to form the Airliner Engineering Corporation in Amityville, Long Island. His first design using the lifting fuselage was the RB-1, an improvement over the flying streetcar but sluggish in turns and lacking good directional control. It was a biplane with a 75-foot wingspan and powered with two Galloway Atlantic engines. The wings were fabric on a wooden frame.

The following design in 1924 was for the RB-2, which had a similar appearance but differed significantly in construction. The RB-2 was a completely metal-covered aircraft with an 18- by 14-foot cabin providing parlor car comfort for 25 passengers. It weighed 5 tons and claimed to be the world's first freight aircraft. In 1925, it demonstrated this capability by carrying an Essex automobile on an aerial sales tour (it was capable of carrying two). It was powered with two Rolls Royce Condor engines. This was the last of the Burnelli biplanes; it was sold to the Aerial Transport Company, with whom it flew freight for eight years before being scrapped.

Burnelli's next design was the CB-16, the first of the monoplanes (one wing) and the first to be built at Aeromarine, where he had rented space. The CB-16's maiden flight was at Newark Airport in 1928, where it was flown by Lieutenant Leigh Wade and Lieutenant James H. Doolittle. In a later flight, the plane lost one engine while carrying a full load of passengers. However, the pilot climbed to 1,000 feet, circled Washington, and landed safely with only one engine. As stated earlier, in a later flight, the plane crashed; the cause was an accidental crossing of the aileron cables. In parallel with the CB-16, Burnelli designed the experimental GX-3 for the 1929 Guggenheim Safe Aircraft Competition. It was an ungainly-looking craft but introduced full span, high lift flaps as well as variable chord and camber. It was too late for the Guggenheim competition but performed well.

The next Burnelli plane was the UB-14, which crashed at Newark Airport, and was replaced by the UB-14B; that story has been told in the previous section. As previously mentioned, the UB-14B had been shipped to Europe, where the Scottish Aircraft & Engineering Company planned to build it. That company then went into receivership. The Cunliffe Owen Company picked up the license to build and produce one British version of the UB-14 in 1938–1939, designated the OA-1. The OA-1 saw service in World War II with the Free French Air Force. The UB-14B, which had been shipped to Europe, was shipped back to the United States and painted red in preparation for the Clyde Pangborn round-the-world flight. However, the flight was cancelled because of the war, and the plane was used for freight service instead.

In parallel with the above, there was a concerted effort by Vincent Burnelli to enter into the competition for production of bombers for the government. While Burnelli was still based in Keyport in 1935, the company entered into the Army Air Corps competitions a design for an A-1 bomber. The design progressed to a partial wooden mock-up, but the Douglas B-18 won the competition. The A-1 bomber design was then modified by Harley Bowlus for General Airborne Transport, Inc. of Los Angeles into a troop or cargo-carrying glider; one was made in 1943.

Effectively, the final chapter in Vincent Burnelli's effort to sell his outstanding lifting-fuselage design occurred in 1942 in the competition for the B-36 bomber contract. He had designed for Canadian Car & Foundry a B-2000B Super Bomber for entry into the competition, and it was a very impressive design. It was so good that it progressed to the point that President Franklin D. Roosevelt was about to sign a contract, per the account of Chalmers H. Goodlin. Burnelli's financial backer was Arthur E. Pew of Philadelphia, who had been a leading supporter of Wendell Willkie in the 1940 campaign. When President Roosevelt asked about Burnelli's financial backing and Pew's name was mentioned, the story goes that Roosevelt threw his pen across the room and tore up the contract. The design was classified secret by the government as a wartime measure and thereby buried from the world for years. Except for a CBY-3 Loadmaster cargo plane, built by Canadian Car & Foundry, which was used for hauling cargo in Venezuela and now sits without engines in the Connecticut Aeronautical Association Museum, the Burnelli Company has not produced any other aircraft. Vincent Burnelli died June 22, 1964.

Aeromarine was a pioneer in many fields of aviation and made itself known throughout the world. There were many significant firsts, both technically and in other accomplishments. In all circles, Aeromarine was recognized as a leader in aviation. The company came very close a number of times to establishing itself as a lasting part of the industry. Many of the designs were superior to those of companies still part of the aviation industry today. Timing and some unfortunate circumstances, however, doomed Aeromarine to failure. It deserves recognition historically, and it is hoped that this chapter will serve that end in some small measure.

Aeromarine ice boat on Raritan Bay. Shown: Joseph Boland (left) and Edwin Musick (right).

11. Prohibition: A Cottage Industry

The temperance movement dates back to the early years of the 1800s with some earlier experiments in prohibition at local levels occurring as early as the 1740s. In the early 1800s, the movement was conducted entirely by men. In the 1850s, women joined the cause, including such noteworthy figures as Susan B. Anthony and later Carry Nation. In November 1874, the National Women's Christian Temperance Union was organized with a goal of legal prohibition of all intoxicating liquor.

In Keyport, the Raritan Temperance Alliance met monthly at various local churches including the First Baptist Church on Main Street and the Methodist Episcopal Church in Mechanicsville. In 1904, the Loyal Temperance Legion was organized under Louisa A. Sands. presidents of groups within the legion included:

The Laurels—Seabrook H. Schanck
The Pansys—Anna Vanderbilt
The Rosebuds—Dorothy Beers
Holy Bible—Cyril Anderson
Sunbeams—Raymond Chinery
Christian Soldiers—Lloyd Armstrong

It is interesting to note that the main supporters of prohibition were the Methodist, Baptist, Presbyterian, and Congregational churches aided by the Disciples of Christ, Christian Science, and Mormon churches. The Methodist churches were the most militant. There were marches as well as meetings including marches down lower Broad Street, where there were many taverns.

There were many attempts made during these years in Congress to amend the Constitution for prohibition of alcohol. The first was introduced in the House in December 1876, followed by others in 1880, 1887, and 1914. The 18th Amendment was adopted by Congress on December 18, 1917. Ratification by the states (33 that were already dry) was accomplished by January 1919, when Nebraska ratified, making it the law of the land on January 16, 1920. In October 1919, the National Prohibition Act (Volstead Act) was passed over the veto of President Wilson. This provided the enforcement machinery for the 18th Amendment and placed its administration under the Bureau of Internal Revenue.

From the moment the 18th Amendment went into effect in January 1920 until it was repealed in December 1933, the prohibition law was broken on a continuous basis. Support for prohibition stemmed from the rural areas. New Jersey in 1910 was one of eight states with 60 percent or more urban population. The Roman Catholic and Jewish faiths were among those that preached temperance but opposed prohibition. New Jersey, in 1916, was one of 19 states where over 45 percent of church members were Roman Catholic or Jewish. The law was very unpopular in New Jersey and was broken by the average citizen. Per Sinclair in his book *Prohibition*:

> a drunken American under prohibition was considered the champion of liberty against tyrannical government. A visit to a cocktail party

Liquor supply ship stationed just outside the 3-mile limit. Ink drawing by Robert Moore.

Boat on Luppatatong Creek typical of those used by rumrunners.

> or a speak-easy became a sign of emancipation, a Purple Heart of individuality in a cowardly and conforming world.

Illegal liquor was supplied to the public in three ways: People made "home brew" or harder spirits, often using the family bathtub and buying supplies and equipment on the open market; stills were set up in hidden locations in the country and inside buildings in towns and cities; and liquor was smuggled into the country.

The last method was called rumrunning and involved smuggling across the Canadian or Mexican border, or from supply ships stationed outside the 3-mile (and later 12-mile) limit in international waters. The larger ones were mostly Canadian or New England fishing schooners that could carry 1,000–3,000 crates on a trip. There were also steam trawlers, converted yachts, tramp steamers, and old windjammers. The ships brought liquor in from Canada, the West Indies, and as traffic increased, from many European countries. Smaller boats would go out from the shore, buy from the supply boats, and run past the Coast Guard to shore. Liquor was often in sacks to permit hiding in compartments and loading in areas not designed for carrying cargo in crates. The sack was also called the "burlock," a package holding six bottles jacketed in straw, three on the bottom, then two, then one, all of which was sewed tightly in burlap.

In the earlier days when Rum Row was just beyond the 3-mile limit, all sorts of boats were used to run liquor from there to the shore. Even hardy souls in rowboats were known to have made the passage. With the change to a 12-mile limit and as the pressure from the Coast Guard increased, larger and faster boats were used. One thing that contributed in large measure to involvement in rumrunning in Keyport and all other bayshore communities was the state ban on oystering and clamming. In November of 1925, New Jersey placed this into effect because of widespread pollution of the water by industry and by local sewer plants. The oystermen and clammers found themselves without a livelihood and with an investment of boats and equipment. Some turned to fishing and some turned to rumrunning. They all knew the waters thoroughly, including the depths of creeks and positions of sand bars. After a load was landed, it would usually be stored in a hiding place on shore (often a cellar or attic of a home) and then transported to buyers in the cities or in some cases directly to speakeasies.

Keyport was well-situated for rumrunning, and many used it in the traffic. In a typical scenario as recounted by Wilbur Huylar, rumrunners would come around East Point (Conaskonk Point), cross Island Bar, and run into Chingarora Creek. The Coast Guard cutters, which in the early years were slower and larger boats, could not cross Island Bar except at high tide. Frustrated in their pursuit, they would fire on the retreating rumrunners with their one-pounders. By the time the Coast Guard was able to follow, the boat would be unloaded and the liquor removed to a safe hiding place.

Many of the vessels used by the rumrunners were built in Keyport. Hulgar Martin Kofoed, who had the Hensler-Kofoed Yacht Basin, built three 50-foot skiffs used by the rumrunners: the *Fleur-de-Lis*, the *Lily of the Valley*, and the

Rumrunner headed for Chingarora Creek with the Coast Guard boat not far behind and firing at him. Ink drawing by Robert Moore.

Wee. These all had a wide beam, curved stem, and were of lapstrake construction (i.e. with the planks in the hull overlapping like clapboards on a house). Kofoed designed and built the hulls; the rumrunners provided the modified aircraft engines. Thanks to Clyde MacKenzie, we understand that the Hensler-Kofoed yards built other boats as well, some 42 feet long and some 56 feet long, and most were painted green. The 56-foot boats had three Liberty engines in them. Some other boats used locally in rumrunning were the *More' La Rue*, the *Adios*, the *Maria*, and the *Ruby*.

The Coast Guard was severely undermanned and its counterparts on land, the Prohibition agents, were not much better off. The rumrunners ran into many creeks, beaches, and inlets along the bayshore, so it was seldom possible to be waiting on land when boats pulled in to be unloaded.

The names of those engaged in the various phases of rumrunning are largely elusive to this day. In the beginning years, there were many local people involved. Later, the gangsters moved in to control the trade, and only a very hardy few remained from the area. Many of those involved prefer to remain anonymous. A few are so well-known that there is no reason not to mention their names in this narrative.

One who was famous locally in the rumrunning trade was "Goody" Johnson, who operated with his brothers and with Pete and Ike Kneute. On one occasion, Goody was returning from a rendezvous with one of the offshore supply ships, when he hit an unseen log. The impact split the prow of his loaded boat wide open. Thinking quickly, he ran the engines at full throttle, which lifted the bow enough to stay afloat long enough to beach the boat. He unloaded quickly by Terry's Boat Yard and left the wreck on the beach.

In another incident off Keyport, the Coast Guard sank the *Cigarette*. The *Cigarette* had been used very successfully in the trade because it could outrun any Coast Guard boat. It was powered by twin Liberty engines normally used for aircraft. In the later years of Prohibition, some of the rumrunners switched to Mack truck engines to be able to haul heavier loads.

All runs were not successful with the rumrunners staying one step ahead of the Coast Guard. Three local men had their boat sink. Joe Hanes and Buck Bennett drowned, and Pet Johnson was rescued after many hours in the water.

There was a violent exchange at the foot of Broad Street by the steamboat docks in 1923. Charles Cogan, a Prohibition officer, contacted Keyport Mayor Thomas L. Smith and told him that a truckload of booze was to pass through Keyport in the area of the docks. Keyport Officers Mason and Coward were detailed to watch for and stop the truck, and they were joined by Prohibition officers. At about 3 a.m., a motorboat landed at the dock and started to unload cases of booze. When the bootleggers saw the Prohibition officers rushing out to apprehend them, they jumped into their boat and sped off. Several shots were then exchanged. One bootlegger was left behind and landed in the water. He later made his escape through the streets of Keyport. There were empty trucks on the dock, and the cases of liquor were taken away.

Scene of the shootout between rumrunners and the Keyport police in 1923.

In November, Prohibition officers captured Pet Johnson and Frank Conklin a short distance offshore from the New York and New Jersey Steamboat Company's dock (at the foot of Broad Street). The authorities seized 100 cases of liquor. The officers were waiting in a boat for their arrival and fired several shots. The bootleggers were unarmed and surrendered. At about the same time, Keyport men were involved in a rumrunning incident across the bay at Lemon Creek, Staten Island. They were smuggling in 83 cases of Scotch in the 40-foot motorboat *Mildred D*. The local people in the crew were William Van Egelen of Keyport and Joseph C. Haynes of Union.

The Coast Guard, in the meantime, was taking other measures to deter the liquor traffic. The Coast Guard cutter *Seneca* had opened fire with its 4-inch gun on the rum fleet anchored outside the 3-mile limit in May of 1923, making the fleet scatter. Shortly later, the Coast Guard seized the British schooner *Tomako*, which had been anchored outside the 3-mile limit. Bill McCoy, the British captain, was taken into custody. These forays by the Coast Guard, however, did not seem to really make a difference in the volume or frequency of the rum traffic.

In February of 1924, a boat with a cargo of 110 cases of mixed liquors was brought ashore at Monmouth Beach. The cargo was believed to be consigned to Keyport, but the boat carrying it was disabled. Four rumrunners may have been drowned off Keyport in the still-frigid March waters of Raritan Bay. They were being chased by New York Police Launch 4, with the launch spraying machine gun bullets at the rumrunners, when the gasoline tank of the 40-foot boat exploded. One of the four fugitives leaped into the water with his clothes ablaze, and the other three occupants followed him. The police searched but found no trace of the men. The blazing boat ran ashore in Union and burned beyond identification.

Only a few weeks later, a boat containing 70 cases of scotch were seized in Keyport harbor by Customs Inspector P.J. MacEvoy and officers of the New York Police Department. The rumrunners seized were Thomas Secondino, the owner of the *Mary, K12118*, and two other men, one of whom was Joe Conwell of Keyport. The police were using one of the New York Police launches and tracking another boat that escaped (under a hail of bullets), when they discovered the *Mary* just inshore from their boat and captured it after firing two shots to prevent its escape. The rum boat was then towed to Perth Amboy to the customs dock. It is interesting to note the teaming in these incidents of Prohibition officers (sometimes referred to as agents), customs inspectors, New York police, and local police officers.

At just about the same time as this last seizure, Keyport police captured whiskey on the beach at the foot of Walnut Street. Officers Mount, Mason, and Coward had been alerted to watch for a landing at that site. They heard a motor running, but before they could determine the precise spot, the rumrunners had landed most of their cargo and then escaped when they heard the police approach. It was alleged that 26 cases were captured but only 6 made it to the Keyport borough hall. In recent years, a secret room with a connecting access to the beach was discovered by the present owners in the house on the west side of Walnut Street. This may be where the missing cases landed.

Four men were rescued by the Coast Guard Cutter *Manhattan* after their boat hit a log and sank near Ambrose Light. James Granato was from Keyport, and the others were from the bayshore area. They said they had been fishing, but a very reliable source reported that they had visited a ship on Rum Row and had procured a cargo of 135 cases of whiskey at $30 per case. They had gone about 6 miles when the collision occurred. After much yelling for an extended time, the *Manhattan's* searchlight found them and they were rescued, but suffered from exposure.

An interesting aside from capture of rumrunners was the arrest in Newark in September 1924 of a gang that was counterfeiting $10 bills. Three of the bills had been presented to the People's National Bank in Keyport just prior, one by a Keyport businessman and two by farmers in the vicinity. The bogus notes had been produced in Providence and sent to New York for distribution. Much of the issue, it was said, found its way to the rum fleet in payment for cargoes.

The Coast Guard presented a very optimistic report in January of 1925. They claimed less than 5,000 cases of liquor were smuggled in 1924 during the holiday season as against approximately 50,000 cases during the holiday season of 1923. This report was from Superintendent Rasmussen of the Fifth Coast

Assembling Liberty engines at Aeromarine. Twin Libertys were the engines of choice for the rumrunners.

Guard District. This district embraces the New Jersey coast from Sandy Hook to Cape May. For the 1924 holiday season, a survey showed an average of 7 ships at anchor on Rum Row against a 1923 average of 40 ships.

One might think that life was relatively safe on the ships of Rum Row outside territorial limits. This was not the case in January of 1925, however. The ships were hit by a fierce gale, and they could not run for port without being seized. The wreckage of one of the ships was found after the storm off Sea Girt with empty liquor cases caught in the tangle of rigging.

Keyport Chief of Police Daniel A. Van Pelt captured a large barrel of whiskey in May 1925 at the foot of Walnut Street. He had been tipped off that whiskey was to be run through the town. While the chief was delivering his papers, he saw a truck on Walnut Street. When he approached, the driver fled, but the chief drove the truck to Schanck's Garage and notified the county prosecutor.

The rum fleet did not always anchor off Sea Bright. The ships would move to other locations along the coast to make the job of enforcement more difficult. There was quite a concentration of them in August 1925. There were four schooners, two of which flew French flags. There were also two steamships of about 4,000 gross tons each. The Coast Guard maintained a picket boat approach to intercept any boats from shore trying to reach the Rum Fleet.

Constable and former Police Chief Daniel A. Van Pelt discovered a Reo Speedwagon truck mired in the mud on Main Street. The road had been excavated for water lines and the heavy rains had softened the earth. Constable Van Pelt stopped to help and detected the odor of liquor. He was unarmed and could not prevent the escape of the men with the truck, but he managed to arrange to seize the truck with its contents.

An amusing account in the *Keyport Weekly* tells of the *New York Graphic*'s exposé of a *New York Daily News* article of December 1926. The account depicts a payment of $200 to Alexander "Goody" Johnson to stage a rumrunning episode for the *Graphic's* photographer. Arrangement was made for empty liquor cases to be taken out to an abandoned ship, the *Richard T. Green*. Goody hired to help him (at $7 per day), Alfred (Pet) Johnson, William (Pickles) Sickles, Isaac Kneute, and Peter Seep, who were all local men. The article states that when the *Graphic* proposed this to him, Goody Johnson replied, "Oh, goody, goody." This supposedly was the basis for his nick-name. The fake pick-up and rumrunning was staged. The *Graphic* reported a fast escape accompanied by the rattle of machine gun bullets. Perhaps just as amusing, however, were the denials of any activity in Keyport by Chief Mount. He said that Rum Row had been smashed two years before (which is inconsistent with all other evidence) and that the participants had not earned anything in the trade for four or five years.

Captain George Mason and Chief Asbury Mount arrested Charles Newman of Atlantic Highlands and seized 72 bottles of liquor and 4 bottles of home brew secreted in an old Dodge car. The incident occurred at the corner of West Front Street and Broadway in December of 1927. By 1929, the 3-mile limit had become the 12-mile limit. The bootleggers were also using radio to warn the rum ships to steam out to sea.

East Point was the center of a great deal of activity in January of 1930. The Coast Guard spotted two rumrunning boats near the point and pursued them. One boat was sunk with its 500 cases of rye; the other boat dumped its cargo of 700 cases and escaped. When the news spread, the area became crowded with hundreds of people seeking liquid salvage. Cases of "Silver Dollar" and "Golden Wedding" were retrieved and sold for $10 to $35 per case. The *Keyport Weekly* commented that "Apparently everyone on shore enjoyed the day and it is safe to say that many called it a holiday. Some are still celebrating." Anita (van Rixoort) Slovenz remembered the excitement of that day with people flocking to East Point. She said many juveniles picked up cases, sold them for $5, and had new bicycles the next day. At about the same time, a truck carrying 184 cases of alcohol was seized at "Five Points" (later referred to as Six Corners) in Keyport. The rumrunners were arrested. One of the rumrunning boats out of Keyport was the *Wee*. Coast Guard Patrol Boat Number 215 chased it in September 1930 but found no alcohol aboard. The *Wee* was often at the Keyport Boat Works for repairs.

In November of 1930, the rumrunners used a false alarm to screen the unloading of liquor from boat to truck in Keyport. The boat had docked by the

Night scene of Johnson's Cove from a painting by Anita Slovenz. Anita's family lived across the street from "Goody" Johnson and it was a common sight to see crates and burlocks unloaded from his boat.

(Front Street) bridge at Matawan Creek full of cases of liquor. The rumrunners proceeded into Keyport with an Auburn car and a truck. When the occupants of the car saw the truck in place, they went to Lockport and set off a false alarm at Second and Waverly Streets. While fire trucks and policemen looked for a fire in Lockport, the rumrunners loaded the truck and drove it over the bridge and out of town.

The van Rixoort family lived in the first house on the north side of Broadway, Union Beach, by Chingarora Creek. The Johnson family, including Goody, lived across the street. When the tide was high, Goody's boats full of liquor could not get under the bridge and trolley trestle. He offered to pay Mr. van Rixoort to use his cellar as a safe haven when the tide was high, but van Rixoort refused. Goody had to continue to carry cases through the van Rixoort yard and across Broadway. The Johnsons had a path running back to a cove where their boats would anchor. Cases of liquor brought in would be loaded on trucks parked on Broadway (Union Beach), often in broad daylight.

Anita also remembered when her Uncle Louis decided to build a boat and do some rumrunning. He wasn't an expert when it came to engines. He had finished the boat and had it in the water near the hulk of the *Bluebird* to test it out on a Sunday. Dominie Reynolds of the Dutch Reformed Church called to him and told him he should be in church. Uncle Louis started the engine anyway, and the boat blew up. He survived, but that was the end of his rumrunning career. She also remembered going to a party given by one of the local police. She was amazed to find that the policeman had a whole attic full of cases of booze. Anita also said that Goody Johnson joined the Coast Guard after the repeal of Prohibition.

With repeal of Prohibition in December 1933, there was still some rumrunning occurring on a modest scale. The federal, state, and local taxes were set so high that the rumrunners found they could make a profit of about $10 per gallon on imported liquor. This persisted well into 1934. In support of this traffic, the Rum Row off the coast changed to very fast, low-lying, Diesel-powered ships. Instead of positioning themselves in one spot, they moved around to confuse the Coast Guard. Furthermore, they were all painted a dirty black to make them as invisible at night as possible.

Some of the boats had other cargo besides rum. On one occasion, a rumrunner was being chased by the Coast Guard around East Point with the Coast Guard gaining. The rumrunner dropped his human cargo overboard, some of whom swam or walked in the shallows to shore. Shortly thereafter, a single file of Chinese aliens walked through Keyport and were apprehended by the authorities. It was believed that others went their separate ways and escaped capture. How much of this traffic there was will probably never be known, but it would appear this was no more than an incidental sideline.

The liquor was stored in many places locally. Many houses in and around Keyport had attics, cellars, and "secret" rooms for hiding illegal beverages until

This was the Barton house where Chief Van Pelt and Officer Mason found George Pease moving cases of booze.

they could be transported to buyers. There was an underground cache at 37 First Street with railroad rails for reinforcement of its roof.

One house on Church Street had a secret loft for such storage that was very well hidden, but the Prohibition officers were suspicious about the house. One day, a shipment of crates had come in and there had not been time to stow it away in the hidden storage area, when the Revenue agents approached the house. They quickly stacked the crates in the shape of a piano, covered them with a sheet, and let the agents in. The place was searched, but they failed to lift the sheet. No liquor was found.

In January of 1925, chief Daniel A. Van Pelt received a tip that George Pease had cases of liquor stored in the Barton House (75 Main Street). Pease, when confronted by Chief Van Pelt, pulled out two or three $500 bills from his pocket and offered to wager it against $2 that he had no liquor in the house. At about 7:30 a.m., the chief spotted Pease behind the house and when he ran in, found him moving cases of booze from a room to the back porch. The liquor seized was in two piles, one of 25 to 30 cases and one of 35 to 45 cases. The chief left officer George "Footsie" Mason to guard the cases from the window of a neighboring house because of the extreme cold. Even though the officer did not leave the window in William Chadwick's house, when the chief returned, most of the liquor had mysteriously disappeared.

There were few who informed on the rumrunners or the storage areas. The law was generally unpopular in the first place. In addition, the people involved were often friends and neighbors. Those who were in the trade were appreciative, and many a milk box yielded a sample bottle or some other token of appreciation from time to time.

State Trooper George Wallis raided a home in Cliffwood and arrested a very resourceful bootlegger. Harold Houston Williams was locked in the jail at Keyport until he could be moved for trial before a federal judge. The next morning when trooper Wallis went to bring food to the prisoner, the cell was empty. He had torn the bunk in the cell apart and used the two-by-fours to pry the cell's bars apart. The outer door was unlocked and he walked out; they never found him.

There were local speakeasies, but the major market for liquor was in the cities. Local law enforcement generally was not a problem for bootleggers, but vehicles suspected of transporting liquor were subject to search and possible seizure by Prohibition officers and state police. As a result, all kinds of vehicles were used for the purpose. Hudson cars brought in for repairs at Buhler & Bitter were found to have double floors in them. In Freehold, a Hudson car was stopped and liquor was seized. The Hudson had compartments under the floor and a fake rear cushion with pockets for the bottles.

Obviously, Hudsons were not the only vehicles that were modified for use in the trade. There were modifications made to many vehicles. Aside from vehicle modifications, there were milk trucks with milk surrounding more expensive liquids. There were even coffins heavily laden with booze. There is, by the way, an interesting rationale put forth for the origin of the word "booze." There was a bottle manufacturer in Perth Amboy during this period whose name, Louis Booz, appeared on his bottles. The bottles were used extensively for the liquor from the numerous stills and for liquor that had been adulterated. After a while, with the name before them on the bottles, the liquor itself became "booze."

Very early in the Prohibition era, Monmouth County organized to set up roadblocks to stem the flow of liquor to the cities. In an operation in November 1923, County Detective Smith and a state trooper stopped every vehicle that passed Browns Point in Keyport from early evening until dawn the next day. They stopped one car from New York that contained a considerable amount of liquor. Also, the police were generally always watching. Local officers chased a speeding sedan on Broad Street in Keyport and found two cases of liquor. The driver was unarmed but said he would have used a gun if he had one.

Local police noticed that a certain Essex coupe made regular trips every Sunday to Cliffwood and Matawan. One Sunday, the driver, Fish Greene of Newark, ran over a cat and the police stopped him. They found a gallon of "razor blade" booze in the rumble seat of the car. The driver remarked, "I knew that cat would cause me hard luck." Later, on paying his fine, he said, "It was that cat or a razor in the wood pile that made me lose that heap of rocks."

Dave Baker tells of a delivery he made to Elizabeth for his mother-in-law, Ma Kneute. One evening, he loaded several gallons of liquor into a car and drove it to the destination given him in Elizabeth. There, the chief of police pulled up and escorted him to another place in Elizabeth. He received payment for his cargo, the chief showed him back to the circle, and he drove home.

The officers on patrol for these vehicles were not always honest. In October 1931, Colonel Schwarzkopf, superintendent of the New Jersey State Police, stated that he had allowed six troopers to quit for taking bribes. There was insufficient evidence to support their trial. The situation was discovered when two troopers, when arresting beer truck drivers, were told that protection had been paid for.

In 1924, Daniel W. Walling Jr. landed in the hospital with a bullet wound in the cheek and neck after an attack by a gang of hijackers. In addition, Nathan Cohen of Perth Amboy, who was visiting Mr. Walling's farm, was severely beaten. Bootleggers had been renting barns from local farmers for storage of their liquor and paying handsomely. In this case, the hijackers arrived at 2 a.m. because they had heard there was a large supply of booze stored in Mr. Walling's barn. They found him asleep in his car, Mr. Cohen nearby, and no cargo of booze. They shot Mr. Walling and beat Mr. Cohen and left. Both were treated by Dr. Peteler of Keyport and then taken to Perth Amboy Hospital.

Charles Monniger of Union Beach posed as a Prohibition agent and stopped to search cars. When the Keyport Borough Clerk, Adelaide Crammer, wrote to the Prohibition office at Newark to inquire about his credentials, the Newark office wrote back to say Monniger had no authority to act in such a capacity.

Monniger seems to have assumed he had the authority to stop vehicles because he provided information to the authorities that led to arrests.

As stated above, most of the booze was transported to the cities. However, Keyport and other communities along the Bayshore had speakeasies as well. The first record of fines levied for operating drinking establishments was a roster of most of the establishments along the "Barbary Coast," a familiar term for many years given to lower Broad Street in Keyport. Fines and jail sentences went to the proprietors of the Bayside Hotel, Raritan Inn, McRann's, Mansion House, and the Monmouth Hotel. The Raritan Inn had a small bar in a hidden basement room. There was even a raid of a lunchroom run by Charles Ross on Second Street in 1924.

Of the above establishments, the Bayside Hotel was the one most frequently raided, nine times from 1920 (mentioned above) to December 1932. Mary Wallace, who was the proprietor of the Bayside Hotel, served jail sentences, paid fines, and even spent time at the State Prison for Women at Clinton. Her husband Jim was raided four times for his place at the corner of First Street and Myrtle Avenue and served several jail sentences. They certainly set a record for persistence. In the chill cold of February 4, 1926, the Bayside Hotel was engulfed in flame during the early morning hours. Mary and James Wallace were in jail, but other members of the family were in the building. The fire department poured volumes of water on the blaze, even cutting a hole in the ice

Keyport's most frequently raided speakeasy. Mary Wallace spent some jail time as a result.

Many stills of all sizes were found in and around Keyport. The one pictured was a small operation. (Pen and ink drawing by Robert Moore)

and pumping bay water on the fire. The fire hoses were coated with ice from the sleet and rain, but the flames were contained and finally extinguished. The building was partially covered by insurance.

It was rebuilt and raided again; after Prohibition, it continued as a bar with a very colorful history. It acquired the nickname "Bucket of Blood" or "Bucket" for short. The clientele were known for their love of a good fight, to such an extent that the nickname was applied. The story goes that one time the patrons even called Earle Naval Ammunition Depot to challenge the marines there to a fight. The "Bucket" finally closed in the early 1990s and remained empty for a while. Very recently, new owners rebuilt the structure and opened it as the Passport Inn.

Authorities returned to the "Barbary Coast" (lower Broad Street) for a massive raid in 1930. In addition to the ever-popular Bayside Hotel, they also raided Melee's Hotel (Monmouth Hotel), Cummings' Hotel, and just outside Keyport on Florence Avenue, the establishment of Mrs. Abe Kanute [sic]. The officers confiscated more than 100 gallons of liquor. In another raid a few months later on Melee's Hotel, kegs of wine and whiskey were seized and removed. It was estimated that within a few minutes of the raiders' departure business resumed. Other speakeasies were closed in anticipation of another raid. It was claimed that the raid was triggered by the hotel's change of a beer supplier.

As stated earlier, some of the illegal liquor was smuggled into the country, but some of it was produced here. Beer was fermented, wine was squeezed and fermented, and other liquors were distilled. Most of the raids were against stills, which could be hidden in the least likely places. Louis Walling, in Keyport, had two stills in operation. One had a capacity of 5 gallons and the other of 20 gallons. Caught with the 5-gallon still working at full capacity, he pleaded guilty following a raid of his premises.

In August 1930, federal officers raided a brewery in the heart of Keyport at 18–24 Broad Street. It was described as one of the largest breweries ever raided in the United States. There were eight 3,000-gallon vats filled with beer and all of the equipment to produce at least 100 barrels a day. The raiders found fully charged ammonia tanks, which they feared might explode. They said that such an explosion would be enough to demolish the entire block.

Even though Prohibition was repealed in December of 1933, the production of illegal liquor went on, and stills continued to be found and raided. After Prohibition ended, Leon Schanck Jr., said he found an abandoned still built into 74 Main Street. A separate water line went around the meter. How long this was in operation, no one knows.

Jimmy Granato lived in Keyport on Broadway. He was said to have been a henchman of Al "Scarface" Capone and that he worked with Capone in the winter of 1930–1931 in Florida. He was believed to have been involved in the slaying of Johnny Goodwin, an alleged narcotics smuggler. He was also a suspected rumrunner. On Saturday morning, December 5, 1931, people living near Broadway and West Front Street were awakened by the sounds of a man screaming early in the morning. One man rushed to a window and another ran out to see what was the matter only to see a car speeding off in the fog. The following day, a man looking for evidence of deer poaching in Brielle found Jimmy Granato in a shallow grave. His body had been soaked with acid. It was believed the murdered man was "bumped off" by members of a rival gang. It was also thought that Jimmy's brother John, who lived in Keansburg, had met the same fate. There were reports, however, that he was alive.

Keyport Police Officer Leroy Sproul arrested Natale Pasino of West Front Street, Keyport, and Frank Monge of Raritan Township. Also apprehended were two men from Oak Shades. The murder was by strangulation and later being shot four times. The authorities believed that it was carefully planned, including digging the grave in advance. Two months later, three more suspects were apprehended in a swamp in Virginia. There is no mention, however, of any indictments following these arrests.

In 1933 also, an autopsy was performed at Bedle's morgue in Keyport on the body of gangster Al Lillien. He had been slain in his mansion in Middletown by an unknown assailant. His bodyguard, and the caretaker of the estate, claimed they had been sent off to Manasquan to wait until Lillien called them, which left Lillien at the mansion alone.

Closer to home, Charles Tourine of Matawan was arrested in Newark. He was charged with the murder of Gustave Berg (a Union City beer runner), two robberies, and was connected with the abduction of Helen Arose of Keyport. Two years before, Helen's mother saw her daughter, who was 17 years old, get into a car with Tourine. The distraught mother swore out a warrant, but Helen Arose was never seen or heard from again.

The "Barbary Coast" (lower Broad Street) in the days before Prohibition.

Harry M. "Stretch" Aumack of Kearney Street in Keyport made a gruesome discovery on his way to work. He was driving out Lloyd Road near the present day Lloyd Road School when he saw a Packard with the headlights on and sitting on the wrong side of the road. As he came abreast of the car, he could see a lot of blood all over the driver, who was slumped over. The victim was identified as "Chee Chee" Santanello, and it was thought that the gangland slaying was related to recent raids on stills or a bootleg feud.

As repeal of Prohibition approached, there was much discussion of how legalized sales of alcoholic beverages would be handled in the post-Prohibition era. In March of 1933, Governor A. Harry Moore expressed his opposition to the sale of beer at bars. He felt it should be confined to restaurants, stores, and hotels. Within the commission appointed by the governor, the prevailing opinion seemed to be that manufacturers, distributors, and wholesalers should be controlled and licensed by the state and retailers should be controlled and licensed by local governments. A special commission sponsored by John D. Rockefeller Jr. proposed the establishment of state liquor stores to sell all hard liquors. The Volstead Act, the basis for enforcement of Prohibition, was modified in April 1933 to permit the sale of light beer and wine. This was the first relaxation of the sale of alcoholic beverages since 1920, when Prohibition began.

At the same time that preparations were being made for the post-Prohibition era, there were still four ships positioned just beyond the 12-mile limit with cargoes of liquor to be run in past Coast Guard vessels. They monitored the operation closely, but every so often a rumrunner would break through. This persisted well into 1934. The reason for the continuance was the high federal, state, and local taxes and fees imposed on legal liquor, which gave the rumrunners a margin of $10 per gallon.

In December 1933, Keyport granted five licenses for sale of liquor, two of which were for consumption off the premises and three for consumption on or off premises. One of these was to Mrs. Jessie Johnson at 188 First Street. This same establishment was later known as Goody and Em's—the same Goody Johnson who was such a successful entrepreneur during the heyday of Prohibition. Later in the same month, more licenses were granted for Raritan Inn, Melee's Monmouth Inn, and Cummings' place, all of which had been raided at one time or another for running speakeasies. The granting of these licenses was criticized as establishing one place for sale of alcoholic beverages for every 500 people in the town. Three ministers protested the granting of some of the licenses because the establishments would be within 200 feet of a church and of a school, but the state commissioners of the Department of Alcoholic Beverage Control ruled that the licenses were legally granted. Keyport with the rest of the country left Prohibition behind and returned to a quieter way of life.

When a thirst persisted and all else failed, one could take an Aeromarine flight to the Caribbean and stop at the Bimini Bay Rod and Gun Club.

12. KEYPORT FILLS OUT

Keyport in its heyday—the shipping center, the boat-building center, the hub for Jersey Central Traction Company, the center for commerce and industry—was a bustling town with dirt roads. It was also a place fed by privately owned toll roads and with three creeks running through it from east to west. Very early there was a bridge across the Luppatatong Creek at Front Street, but for many years there was a demand for a bridge across the Luppatatong at Mott Street (now Maple Place). In 1900, Freeholder John W. Keough managed to obtain county funds for a bridge, and it was completed by September of that year (in 1951, the bridge was replaced with a causeway). At the same time, Keough pushed through funding for a stone road from Keyport to Keansburg. There was also pressure for conversion by the county of toll roads, such as the Keyport-Holmdel Turnpike, to public roads and building a stone road to South Amboy.

By June 1900, First Street had been widened from 33 to 43 feet and Second Street had been extended to connect with Stone Road to the east. By August 1900, the portion of the Freehold-Keyport Turnpike between Keyport and Matawan Station was condemned and declared a public road. In May 1901, the Freeholders voted funds to purchase the Middletown-Keyport Turnpike and the Keyport-Holmdel Turnpike. All toll houses were closed except one in June 1901. Homer B. Anderson had completed just short of 21 years as toll taker at Hazlet.

Dirt roads were dusty in dry weather. Abram Morris Jr. used a fine new Studebaker sprinkling cart in June 1901 to alleviate the problem. It was also common practice to spray oil on the roads. In rainy weather, they became impassable seas of mud. In March 1902, Broad Street from Mechanicsville to the railroad track (Butler Street) was so bad it was closed to the public. This situation was no better in wet weather as late as March 1910. In June 1913, work started on Broad Street from the railroad crossing to Front Street to rebuild the roadway. Stone roads were better, but nothing like the roads of today. Traffic could use a stone road in wet weather, but pedestrians still had to wade through a muddy morass to cross.

The railroad crossed Mott Street at an angle between Osborn and Atlantic Streets and the railroad built a picket fence along its right of way in October

1903, blocking off Mott Street. The matter was taken to court, and on June 16, 1905, the court ruled that the fence must be removed. In 1906, hearings were held with the Army Corps of Engineers and the County Freeholders concerning the Oyster (Luppatatong) Creek bridge. The old bridge was found to be in deplorable condition, and a new iron bridge was erected 8 feet over mean high water. Traffic was interrupted for only four hours!

In January 1908, the state of New Jersey decided to build a stone road between South Amboy and Keyport with a goal of completion by the end of the year, yet it was not finished until July of 1909. This link tied traffic from New York and northern New Jersey to the Jersey shore through Keyport at West Front Street, which was called Bridge Street between Matawan Creek and Broadway. In November 1912, per Keyport's request, Monmouth County accepted Broad Street between Front and First Streets as part of county roads, completing the link for shore traffic through Keyport. For many years, this was the only highway; it brought business to Keyport, but also a tremendous amount of traffic. A report of conditions in the *Keyport Weekly* indicates how heavy. On July 15, 1922, the return traffic was so slow that it was estimated that "as many as 2400 automobiles passed Broad Street corner in a single hour." A survey taken in August 1923 recorded that several thousand vehicles passed the corner in a 72-hour period. In December 1919, the Freeholders decided to make First Street (part of the highway) a cement road and later extend the

The Mott Street bridge. Mott Street later became Maple Place, and the bridge was replaced by a causeway.

cement roadway to Keansburg. In 1923, the county accepted jurisdiction over First Street in exchange for Second Street, which became a borough street.

The heavy shore traffic forced the state to consider alternatives. In 1928, it decided to bypass Keyport's downtown and build a road across the Cliffwood meadows and a new highway bridge. In August, the first steel was placed on the bridge, but the approaches across the meadows seemed to have no bottom and took a long time. After this bypass was completed and in service, traffic flowed through the outskirts of Keyport, but there was a natural bottleneck—Six Corners. Broadway, Maple Place, and the highway met there with a traffic light. The problem persisted through 1951, when a two-way light plan was considered and rejected. Finally in 1961, the state built an overpass to carry all traffic over the highway.

While highways were being built, Keyport's local roads were being paved. In addition to First, Second, part of Broad, and Front Streets, the county paved Maple Place and Broadway with cement. The borough paved Walnut Street (to support Aeromarine traffic) and part of Church Street with cement. Through the 1920s, most of the Keyport streets were paved with macadam. Almost all remaining unpaved streets were macadamized in the 1930s and Atlantic Street from Highway 36 to Maple Place in the 1940s.

Keyport's first school was built on Church Street on a lot donated by the Keyport Company. The Methodist Church was built on the same property, and the school bought it from them in 1856. Even the church building constituted cramped quarters, so in 1871–1872, a new brick school was constructed on the Broad-Maple-Division-Elizabeth block. This was added on to in 1892 and 1912, and in 1880 a high school was established in the same building. The first graduating class had only one graduate, Frank VanBrakle. By 1923, the graduates had increased to 23, and the ceremonies were held in the armory. Starting in 1905, there was pressure for building primary schools in Lockport and Browns Point, and they were built in 1908 and 1909. The Lockport school today is a senior center. In 1911, central heat was installed in the grammar school, and in 1912 under pressure from the state, Keyport had to improve classroom lighting, improve the heating system, make stairwells fireproof, install inside toilet facilities instead of outhouses, add to the building, and replace the shingle roof with slate. The voters approved the budget, and the changes were made for $40,000. High school graduates totaled 13 in 1914 and 11 in 1916.

In 1924, St. Joseph's Parochial School was dedicated, which provided a second grammar school in Keyport. At the same time, it was proposed that a new public high school be built. There were only six teachers in the high school to teach 197 students. On June 30, 1925, the proposition was placed before voters and rejected. The need was recognized by 1928, and the cornerstone for a new building was laid on June 9, 1928. In 1937, the federal Work Projects Administration (WPA) built a manual training addition to the building. In addition, WPA provided an athletic field for the high school. The WPA was a make-work program established to provide employment during the Depression by financing and building public facilities.

The toll house for the Keyport-Holmdel Turnpike located at the corner of Atlantic and South Main Streets. The pond next to it, despite rumors, was not called Aumack's Pond; Aumack's Pond was across present day Florence Avenue near Middle Road.

From 1830 to 1891, all water came from private wells. Lots were in most cases 50 feet or less in width and often only 100 feet deep. Wells were dug and lined with brick, therefore only tapping surface water. In addition, houses had "honey suckle cottages"—outhouses—behind them. The ground was becoming polluted. In addition, even though the only fire company was a hook and ladder company, there was no central source of water for fighting fires. In 1889, a second great fire occurred in the business section.

In February 1891, the town commissioners called a special election on March 31 to consider establishing a central water system. By April, the artesian well had been drilled on the Wygant property near the bay, and the water had been tested. On March 4, 1893, the borough bought a lot on the corner of Church and Elizabeth Streets to erect a standpipe for water storage and pressure. There was a Women's Christian Temperance Union (WCTU) drinking fountain at Broad and Front Streets and a fountain by the well in Lockport.

By August 1901, water mains had been laid throughout town and were being extended up Beers Street to the tile factory. In August 1909, the borough (Keyport became a borough in 1908) arranged to clean the standpipe, but purification of the water did not arrive until 1913. Use was by water rents, a flat

Keyport Yacht Club seen from the dock. The white arch on shore was a lime kiln.

charge per house. In August 1925, $13,000 was due the borough for water rents. In 1928, a new pumping station was built at the base of Cedar Street.

No action was taken to install a sewer system until 1910. In April, a map of a proposed system was prepared, and in September, the people voted to proceed. The Harrison Construction Company was selected, and installation began in November 1910. Except for manhole explosions when someone tried to burn off excess gases by dropping a lighted newspaper into a manhole and the need to relay pipe from one section laid on pilings, the installation of the sewer system proceeded very smoothly. It was accepted in December 1912.

The "filling out" of Keyport wasn't all schools, roads, and facilities as Keyport matured in many other ways. In 1890, people organized the Keyport Brass Band, which was a source of pride and pleasure in the area for about two decades. In May 1903, Broadway Park opened near the (old) car barn with a dance pavilion, a baseball field, and a carousel. Regular baseball games were played there. By July, a shooting gallery had been added and a shuffleboard court and photo gallery planned. Pavilion Beach on the waterfront provided the other center for entertainment; by July 1903, they were showing moving pictures. In August 1903, Broadway Park was advertising animated pictures of the President McKinley funeral.

Pavilion Beach opened as an amusement park on June 27,1903. There was a large open pavilion with many seats for concerts, moving pictures, and light vaudeville. It was here that Fred Astaire and his sister Adele made their professional debut. In September 1903 and September 1904, the facility was closed for non-payment of bills. In 1905, Frank J. Knapp leased Pavilion Beach and ran it efficiently for several years. It was described as a veritable Coney Island. There were amusement stands, a skating rink, bath houses, and boat rentals. The competition at Armory Theater introduced basketball games, roller skating, moving pictures, vaudeville, and even burlesque. In December 1910, the car barn by Broadway Theater was converted into an opera house.

Outside these places of entertainment, the Keyport Yacht Club was organized in May 1910; for three years prior it had operated as the Keyport Boat Club. The Keyport Band had started the Keyport Carnival about 1900, and these extravaganzas continued over the years, usually in August. There were domino tourneys, and Edward Snyder had a large gas light erected in front of his First Street Ice Cream Saloon. (In the early 1930s, Tracy toured the town with his pony-drawn ice cream cart on summer evenings.) In 1909, the council moved to ban slot machines (the 5¢ slots were viewed as particularly insidious).

In 1912, a new 40- by 120-foot building was erected on Front Street and opened on December 23 as the Surf Theater. On the opening night, it was a sell out for two performances. It survived all of the competition and later changed its name to the Strand. In 1913, however, the Armory Theater was the first to show movies with sound. The Armory became the Palace in 1926, and moved from the First Street end of the building to the Front Street end. They added a marquee as well. In 1912, Pavilion Beach became Beach Park, Keyport's first park. It continued as a very popular park for part of the time under the guidance of Alma Lockwood, a local schoolteacher. Finally in 1923, Beach Park was purchased by the borough.

Perhaps the most popular lodge in Keyport was Red Men's Hall; its Scheyichbi Council dressed as Indians and held pow-wows with other councils. Also in Keyport were: Royal Arcanum, GAR, Odd Fellows, Junior Mechanics, Elks, Colored Knights of Pythias, and the Masons. In 1926, the Masons bought the Templeton mansion and property on Third Street to convert to a temple. For a

The baseball field at Broadway Park. This was a magnet on Carnival days and holidays.

while in the early 1930s they had a miniature golf course on their property.

Keyport had its share of people with a claim to fame. One of these was Garrett A. Hobart, who was Vice President of the United States under President McKinley. When he was a small boy, his father moved the family to Keyport and opened a general store as De Forest and Hobart. The family was related to the Hoffs, who were early settlers in Keyport. The Hobarts moved elsewhere and lived in several towns, but Keyport named one of its streets after him.

Georg J. Lober was a famous sculptor, who was born in Chicago in 1892 but adopted Keyport as his home in 1905. His first works of note in 1909 were bas reliefs of Robert Fulton and Henry Hudson. In 1912, he designed the emblem for the Danish National Park at Reabild, Denmark. His bronze statue of Eve was on display at the New York World's Fair in 1939 when it was destroyed by vandals. His bronze relief of Abraham Lincoln is in Rebild Park in Denmark and his portrait of Hans Christian Andersen at the Odense Museum. In 1949, he sculpted the statue of Thomas Paine, which is in Burnham Park in Morristown. In 1950, he was awarded the Knight Cross of the Order of Daneborg, Denmark's highest medal. His 7-foot statue of Hans Christian Andersen is in Central Park. He served for several years as executive secretary of the New York Municipal Art Commission. He died in 1961 and is buried in St. Joseph's Cemetery in Keyport.

Henry E. Ackerson, who made his home in Keyport, served two terms in the New Jersey Senate and was then appointed to the Court of Errors and Appeals. In 1924, he was appointed to the New Jersey Circuit Court and later to the New Jersey Supreme Court.

Juanita Long Hall was a Keyport native and first gained fame arranging and co-directing the play "Green Pastures." She appeared at the New York World's Fair for its entire run with her Juanita Hall Singers. She gained enduring fame in 1949 playing the role of Bloody Mary in "South Pacific." A biographical sketch of her appeared in the June 6 edition of *Time* magazine. She received a Tony award for her performance in April 1950. She never forgot her Keyport roots and put on a concert to raise funds for high school band uniforms in 1954 and a benefit performance for the Second Baptist Church in 1959. In 1959, she played in "Flower Drum Song." She died in 1968 and is buried in Matawan.

Another show business personality made his home in Keyport. George Thornton had an extensive career on Broadway, in road shows, and in the movies. His most famous role was as Grumpy in "Snow White and the Seven Dwarfs" on stage.

Moe Jaffe was a Keyport native who wrote several hit songs. Some of his best known were: "Gypsy in My Soul," "If You Are But a Dream," and "I'm My Own Grandpa." William Bedle's name is not well known, but his invention stands out. A talented wood worker, he invented the Lazy Susan. George Washington Walling was the earliest Keyporter to gain fame beyond the borders of Keyport. He served in the New York Police Department for 38 years and retired as Chief of Police in 1885.

The Surf Theater, which later became the Strand Theater, and is now the Bulkhead Bar and Restaurant.

During the early 1900s, a number of things were proposed or almost happened, which would have changed Keyport a great deal. One of these was the proposal by Councilman Frederick Tibbetts in 1939 to build a dam and sluiceway essentially from near Beers Street to Brown's Point to create a lake covering the meadows along Luppatatong Creek. It was proposed as a National Youth Administration (NYA) project. Two other councilmen opposed it, however, and drummed up enough opposition that the NYA was unwilling to proceed with the project.

A proposal that would have created a smaller lake on the same meadows was proposed by the father of the author, Howard T. Jeandron, in 1950. The county had plans to replace the Maple Place bridge with a causeway. Instead, Howard, for the Keyport Planning Board, proposed making the project a combination causeway and spillway. The county rejected the idea, because it was felt an additional retaining wall would have to be built at the southern end of such a lake to prevent washout of Highway 35.

One project would have been outside of Keyport. E. Donald Sterner, Monmouth County Planning Board chairman, proposed building a bridge from Staten Island to Conaskonk Point to provide an alternate route for shore traffic. The Port Authority opposed it and declared that such a project was within its jurisdiction to adopt or reject.

Another proposal involving Conaskonk Point was to build a nuclear reactor there. Jersey Central Power & Light developed serious plans to build one; a contract to purchase the tract from Union Beach was signed in April 1967. The company subsequently dropped plans for the nuclear plant and then also for an oil-fired plant.

When the old grammar school on the block surrounded by Broad, Elizabeth, and Division Streets and Maple Place was up for sale by the school board, Frank Flynn proposed purchase by the borough governing body and the building of a borough hall on the site. Mr. Flynn, then the building inspector, also suggested a central fire department building on the site. The mayor and council rejected the suggestion.

Finally, the residents of Oak Shades (on Keyport's south-west border) asked to become part of Keyport. The borough was receptive, but opposition from Matawan Township was too strong for the Oak Shades residents to overcome.

This view of Pavilion Beach shows the open-air theater where Fred and Adele Astair made their professional debut.

13. The Years Since Then

In the 1950s, New Jersey extended the Garden State Parkway south of the Raritan River, eventually reaching Cape May. This opened up all areas along its route to development; suddenly the Jersey shore became readily available. The towns reacted in different ways, and their vulnerability depended largely upon the individual zoning ordinances. Hazlet and Matawan Township were swallowed by development overnight. Holmdel changed to 1-acre zoning and, after one housing development, stopped further massive development. Keyport and the other bayshore communities had no large open lands; the effects on these communities were more subtle.

The Keyport School Board was far-sighted in buying in 1949–1950 a large tract between Broad and Atlantic Streets near the high school. It was used in 1958–1959 to build a new grammar school to replace the old (1871–1872) grammar school, which was a fire trap. The new school was enlarged in 1966–1967 and again in 1999. For many years, Keyport High School had Union Beach, Raritan (Hazlet), and part of Holmdel as sending districts—i.e. their students attended Keyport High, and the costs were reimbursed by the sending districts. The high school was enlarged with a new wing in 1952–1953. In 1954 and again in 1959, discussions were started with other towns to consider establishing a regional school system, but by 1964 the regional approach was abandoned. In 1957, Keyport tried without success to exclude Raritan students. Raritan's population had doubled from 1950 to 1956; Superintendent of Schools John O. Hartzler projected a steady increase for the high school of 20 students per month and a need for double sessions. The problem was alleviated when in January 1960 Raritan and Holmdel approved the building of new high schools.

In the meantime, although Keyport had no large areas for development, there were tracts large enough for building apartments. By 1963, Keyport had approved the Betsy Ross apartment complex in south Keyport and was discussing a 140-unit complex on Atlantic Street. These were followed by apartments on Beers Street and Green Grove Avenue and a reduction in the ordinance of square footage required per apartment. The borough government was anxious to add more ratables. Ratables are the amounts assessed for properties within a municipality. The total ratables determine the tax revenue and the amount that can be borrowed. The school board expressed concern to the borough council about the impact of the new apartments on the school program as early as March 1963, and by August projected a need to go on double sessions in the high school. The need for an addition to the high school was evident and was estimated at $519,517 by December. The addition was voted down twice before it was approved in December 1964. In 1965, the school board requested that Monmouth County build a vocational school in Keyport. Approval came in 1966, and it was built within the school complex.

The supply of potable water was also affected by the building of the Garden State Parkway and the resultant expansion of population. Keyport drilled new artesian wells in 1939, 1955, and 1970. Other water companies in the area had to expand in order to cope with increased consumption. In 1959, Keyport Councilman Alton D. Walling reported that Keyport was losing 350,000 gallons of water a day. Some leaks were found quickly and repaired, but resolution of this problem extended over several years. In 1955, Monmouth County announced a plan to restore mill ponds to add to the total water supply. However, nothing much came of the plan. To cope with the building of garden apartments, Keyport had to install a new water pump in 1964. In 1968, after Keyport stopped supplying water to Union Beach and parts of Hazlet and Matawan Townships, the state directed Keyport to build a new water tower to double its storage capacity. In 1972, the borough successfully applied for a Housing and Urban Development (HUD) grant to build the tower, modernize the water plant, and replace old water lines. The grant required matching funds from Keyport.

In the 1980s, the Manasquan Reservoir and New Jersey Water Supply Authority were established. The new reservoir provided a water supply for southern Monmouth County but did not provide for a trunk to supply water to the northern part of the county. In 1989, Shorelands, a private water company, charged that Keyport was destroying the Potomac-Raritan-Magothy aquifer by pumping its complete requirements from it. Keyport had discussed establishing a local reservoir with Matawan by using Lake Lefferts. Keyport also proposed buying water from Old Bridge—at a lower rate. In June 1990, per state mandate, Keyport reluctantly agreed to buy half of its requirements from New Jersey–American Water Company via Shorelands Water Company. In 1993, an attempt was made to sell the Keyport water system, but the move was voted down. In 1992, the Union Beach water system had been sold after voter approval, and Highlands water system was also sold after voter approval. In 1996, 1997, and 2000, Keyport leased the use of the water tower for cellular antenna use. The income from this is $100,000 per year. In March 2003, the mayor and council again announced the intention to sell the water system.

The Raritan Bay out from the shores of Keyport had been a mecca for all interested in swimming, boating, and fishing for countless years. In 1953, the

The waterfront road is American Legion Drive but informally referred to as Ring Road.

state proposed building the Raritan Valley Trunk Sewer to process the domestic and industrial wastes for the Raritan Valley and carry the effluent into Raritan Bay 5 miles beyond the Amboys. There were many complaints about the outfall, but it was built anyway. In June 1953, the state complained that Keyport's sewer plant was not effective. In 1955, Raritan Township complained about pollution caused by Keyport. In response in 1956, Keyport's Mayor Applegate proposed the establishment of a Sewer Authority. As the ordinance was introduced to establish the authority, New Jersey also sent a directive to show cause why the sewer plant should not be shut down. After proposing the authority, Mayor Applegate vetoed the ordinance, saying that renovation of the plant could be accomplished without the authority for much less money. The council overrode the veto, appointed the members, moved to transfer the sewer plant to the authority, and in April 1958 sent the plans for enlargement and improvement of the system to the state. The state approved the plans in July 1958, but when the authority announced the fee schedule for financing all work, the people revolted. There were demonstrations in the streets (including an outhouse on a flatbed truck) because the people felt that the fee schedule was unfair. The council asked the authority to dissolve in July 1958, but the authority did not close until September 1959. At that time, rehabilitation of the plant was estimated at $225,000. The state approved preliminary plans in May 1960, issued a timetable, and approved the final plans in October 1960.

The Keyport Weekly *was the borough's paper from 1869 to 1973. The building shown was its home for most of those years.*

Keyport immediately approved a bond issue to cover the work and named E.T. Killam as associate engineer. At about this time, Union Beach, a neighboring community, applied for federal aid for surveying its sewer needs; it had no sewers at all. The Keyport bids came in $70,878 higher than projections, but award was made to Thomas Procter Company. Keyport had complied with requirements by 1962.

In November 1964, Monmouth County announced a plan for a regional sewerage authority to include Union Beach, Matawan, Matawan Township (Aberdeen), Raritan (Hazlet), and Holmdel. In March 1966, New Jersey changed the rules; all sewer plants were now required to provide secondary treatment. The completed Keyport plant provided only primary treatment. Monmouth County required that all sewerage facilities comply with their master plan and asked for a new survey for Keyport and Matawan. New Jersey gave a very short deadline for Keyport and Matawan to provide plans for secondary treatment. On top of the above, in June 1967, the U.S. Department of the Interior placed a requirement to remove 90 percent of effluents from the waters; this increased the requirement by 10 percent and made all ongoing plans obsolete. In 1968, Monmouth County recommended an outfall into the ocean and asked the state to build it; by 1969, the state had begun to comply.

While Keyport and Matawan were meeting initial requirements and struggling to comply with changing requirements, Union Beach, Raritan, and Holmdel started with only septic tanks and then were locked in to a regional plant mandated by the County—Union Beach reluctantly so. These towns were polluting the bay via seepage into the creeks, while Keyport partially processed effluents with its upgraded sewer plant. Keyport and Matawan tried to gain approvals and financial aid to build their own regional. Finally in 1973, one year after work was started on the Bayshore Regional Sewer in Union Beach, Keyport was forced into using Bayshore as a customer. There was no opportunity for Keyport to become a voting member of the Bayshore authority.

Keyport's primary asset has always been a waterfront with a beautiful view across Raritan Bay to Staten Island and Manhattan in the distance. Until 1923, when Beach Park was purchased, none of that waterfront belonged to Keyport. Then the former Terry Shipyard property was acquired through tax foreclosure, and the waterfront property just east of Lupatatong Creek was acquired from J. & J.W. Ellsworth. The Ellsworth property was bulkheaded and filled in 1950–1951. The former Weigant tract adjacent to the original water works was purchased in 1960. The Harbor Commission was established in 1937 as the Marine Improvement Commission.

As early as December 1951, the Planning Board proposed building a waterfront road behind the stores in the business section. In 1957, Consulting Engineer Louis Booz drew up a plan for bulkheading and filling from Broad Street to approximately Beers Street and the borough-owned former Ellsworth property. Based on later plans by a Newark consulting firm, land was acquired, funds were provided by bonding and a state grant in 1966, and the Erickson property adjoining it was purchased in 1969. Work began that same year, and the present post office building was erected as part of the overall project. It was completed during the Robert Strang administration, and a fishing dock was added during the William Ralph administration. In 1987, ferry service was established from the fishing dock to New York. The service, by Direct Line and later TNT Hydrolines, ran until July 1990 when it suddenly terminated.

In 1971, the Independent Party was organized in Keyport. William Ralph ran for mayor as an Independent against Republican and Democratic candidates and won by a landslide. Ralph endorsed one Republican candidate and one Democratic candidate and they also were elected. The Independents provided a very popular government for about eight years, and then Keyport returned to a two-party system. During the Ralph administration, they designated Keyport the "Gateway to the Bayshore" and painted this on the water tower (at no cost) for all to see.

Politics aside, nature provided an interesting development in 1986. The people of Keyport were able to forget about water bills, sewer bills, politics, and schools. They could simply enjoy an unusual quirk of nature. Parrots started to be seen in the wild near Kearney Street in 1986. They later moved to the area of East Front Street and announced their presence by shrill squawks. They not only survived the winters but also multiplied. Unfortunately, someone captured the younger birds and reduced their numbers to two again. They still survive here in the wild.

In 1973, a waterfront tract was purchased from the New Point Comfort Beach Company (the steamboat docks) for a marina, which was never built. A building on the property was leased in 1974 to the Keyport Historical Society for conversion into the Steamboat Dock Museum. The museum opened in 1976 and has served the public for over 26 years. In 1984, Mayor Richard Bergen contracted building a boat ramp, completed in 1986 after his death. Also in 1984, a citizens' committee working with a borough contractor proposed relocating American Legion Drive to make it an extension of First Street running behind the stores. Several years and administrations later, Keyport is still striving for this concept. In May 1985, the borough decided to accept an offer from Earl Swift for borough garages on a rental basis on Francis Street in order to vacate the public works facility on the waterfront. The Keyport Public Works Department occupied it in 1987, and it is still in use. However, in 2003 the borough purchased property for a new Public Works facility.

The superintendent of public works was Arthur Rooke, who had started as a laborer in the department 25 years before. Under his quiet but efficient management, public works took on, besides water and sewer systems and

Bill Ralph's Independent Party. Shown are: seated from left Howard T. Jeandron, Mayor Ralph, Councilman Donald Redmond. Standing from left Councilman Donald Miller and Julius Rosato.

roads, recycling and maintaining parks and public buildings. When Mayor John Merla presented him with road paving machines, he had his department paving roads. Most towns contract out road paving at a much higher cost. Art's favorite place when off duty was the Keyport waterfront. As a member of the Planning Board, he had had discussions with the U.S. Corps of Engineers about his dream for Keyport—a breakwater extending from Conaskonk Point. He saw that a breakwater was the one way to make the Keyport harbor as good as it was in the glory days of the steamboats. In December 2000, Art Rooke died at the age of 56 and has been sorely missed. Mayor John Merla plans to pursue Art's dream of a breakwater with the Corps of Engineers.

In May 1989, the borough asked the Board of Education to donate the former East Keyport school for use as a senior center. In October, the borough received a Small Cities grant to purchase and renovate a building for the purpose. It was purchased in September 1990, renovated, and opened in June 1992. It has been well received and in 2002 celebrated its tenth anniversary.

Just as part of Keyport's history—a three-room school—had been preserved as a senior center, another part of Keyport's history was about to disappear. Rail service on a line from Matawan through Keyport to Atlantic Highlands dated back to 1889. Later that line was extended to run through Sea Bright to connect again with the main line at West End, Long Branch. Keyport commuters and others used the line regularly. By the early 1950s, the Central Railroad started to cut back on service for this line. In 1953, Keyport's Mayor Herbert Rothenberg voiced opposition to cutbacks. The railroad switched to Bud cars as an economy measure in 1956 and cut off the section from Highlands to Atlantic Highlands in 1958. A Bud car is both passenger car and engine and is normally used by itself to provide limited passenger service for the railroads. All rail service on the Bayshore line was discontinued in June 1972 following the bankruptcy of the Central Railroad. Monmouth County immediately moved to stop any sale of the right of way, later arranged to acquire title, and established the Henry Hudson Trail as a county park running from Keyport to Atlantic Highlands.

Keyport had gained a senior center and part of an unusual county park but still needed an adequate borough hall. Keyport's first borough hall was shared with Hook & Ladder Company on East Front Street. Over the years, the governing body looked for a new site. One of those sites, in 1940, was at 80 West Front Street—two doors from where a new borough hall is being built now. In July 1951, the council bought the vacated Jersey Central Power & Light building at 18–20 Main Street for a borough hall. Renovation had to wait until April 1952, when Jersey Central vacated the building. By the 1980s, the building had been outgrown and, since it is not handicap-accessible, was no longer acceptable for the purpose. In May 1987, fire destroyed a store around the corner from the borough hall, and despite pressures, the owner failed to clear the debris. A facelift of the former Jersey Central building involving façade painting and the addition of awnings in 1989 served only to dress up the outside.

In December 1989, the jail cells were ruled inadequate by the State Department of Corrections. The borough considered various sites around town and by 1994 determined that a new building would be built in the downtown area, but it took until May 1997 to decide that the best site was around the corner where the store had burned ten years before. The land was procured through condemnation in December 1997 and the remains of the burned store bulldozed in April 1998. When bids were received for the new borough hall in August 2000 the low bid was challenged by another bidder. The borough lowered the requirements and put it up for bid again. The second low bidder was also challenged, the challenge went through the courts, and finally in March 2002, the New Jersey Supreme Court ruled in Keyport's favor. Construction started and is now well on the way.

Over the years, Keyport has been hit by several severe storms, some that have altered the course of history. The hurricane of September 1944 inflicted severe damage to the steamboat docks and destroyed several smaller boats. A November 1950 hurricane completed the destruction of the steamboat docks and beached the *City of New York* so that it had to be sold for salvage. The worst storm to hit Keyport, however, was Hurricane Donna in September 1960. It washed over First Street at Beach Park and over West Front Street from about Beers Street to Luppatatong Creek. It knocked out electricity and destroyed a wall of the sewer plant. Damage was widespread in the area, and the cost was estimated in the millions. Since then, the worst storm was a nor'easter in December 1992, which almost destroyed the Steamboat Dock Museum but confined its damage to the waterfront in the business section.

Retrenchment was not all due to storms. By the 1940s, the Strand Theater (formerly the Surf) was Keyport's only movie theater. With television in most homes by the 1950s, the Strand turned into a theater for foreign and avant-garde films and then into a theater for X-rated films. In June 1970, the Strand showed the film *Man and Wife*, and the Keyport police raided the theater and confiscated the film. In March 1973, the police raided again and confiscated *Deep Throat* and *Love for Sale*. A month later, the U.S. District Court ruled that local authorities must desist from seizing the films and allow the theaters to open. The theater stayed open for a few years more and then closed. It re-opened to show older movies that would be acceptable to the general public. Within a year, after many showings with about six people in the audience, the Strand closed its doors permanently.

The *Keyport Weekly* had been publishing local news since 1869. A detailed history of Keyport unfolded in a series by Josephine Brown in the *Weekly* in the 1930s. In addition, the panorama of Keyport history was captured as it occurred with editor J. Mabel Brown at the helm for 50 years of that time. From the 1920s to the 1940s, Brown's brother Herbert published the *Keyport Enterprise*, which covered the news in the same depth and quality. When he died in 1948, the *Weekly* bought the *Enterprise*. In December 1971, the *Weekly* was sold to Shore Publishers, who continued publishing it for two more years before ending its long run.

The plans for the Garden State Parkway included a Keyport exit to spill into Highways 35 and 36 where they joined. The property most affected by this plan was the Winfield Maurer farm. During the discussions between parkway representatives and property owners, the use of the Maurer farm as a shopping center was a focal point. If it had become a shopping center, it might well have been a rival for the Monmouth Shopping Center that was built near the Long Branch exit to the parkway.

The police story for this period began with the early retirement of Chief Michael Kelley in January 1988. The mayor and council provisionally appointed Raymond Lee as his successor pending his passing the civil service exam. Captain Howard Ruth and Sergeant Albert Hafner filed for the exam as well. In June, Chief Lee suspended Captain Ruth for failure to attend a public police inspection. In October, the exam results were released, and showed identical scores for Captain Ruth, a veteran, and Chief Lee, a non-veteran. Civil service rules mandate that when a veteran places highest, he must be appointed. In December, claiming that Ruth could not handle the stress of the job, the council appointed Lee as chief. In March 1989, the state questioned the appointment, and Lee countered with the charge that the test, which included an oral exam,

The City of New York *was driven up on land by the unnamed hurricane of November 1950.*

was biased. Ruth filed an appeal. In September, the state review board voted to disqualify Ruth. He appealed, and the council dropped their opposition to Ruth. Actions went back and forth with actions, suits, and tentative decisions until an administrative law judge in September 1993 declared that charges against Ruth were unfounded. Howard Ruth was appointed as chief in November. Both Lee and Ruth filed lawsuits against Keyport claiming that their rights were violated. In March 1995, Chief Ruth announced he would retire in July 1996, and the borough settled his lawsuit. In April, ex-chief Lee announced retirement, and the borough settled with him.

Prior to Chief Ruth's retirement, the council began to talk about establishing a position of police director instead of selecting a police chief. In July 1996, Keyport established the position of police director. In December 1996, Keyport picked Frank Miele, a retired state police captain, to fill the post of police director. He overcame the feelings of resentment in the department, inculcated a feeling of esprit de corps similar to what he had known as a state trooper, and brought pressure to obtain decent quarters for the department. When he succumbed to cancer in March 2000, he was mourned by everyone in the department and by the entire borough. He had made a difference. In June 2000, the borough decided to restore the position of chief, and in September selected Captain Theodore Gajewski to fill the post.

While the battle was being waged for police chief, the mayor and council examined another possibility. Starting in December 1990, they considered regionalizing by combining the Keyport police department with that of Union Beach. In January 1991, Union Beach authorized a joint study. Keyport also agreed to a study, which was conducted by Leo A. Culloo of Police Management Consulting Services. By May of 1992, both towns agreed that the merger was not feasible. Consolidation of inspection services was tried, however, but abandoned after discouraging results.

In February 1988, Keyport received a state grant for neighborhood preservation. In a public meeting, it was agreed that the money received would be split between the residential and business parts of the designated district. Houses in need of repair were renovated, and the business district was given a face lift. Business owners augmented the state grant money to replace sidewalks and curbs, and the county repaved Front Street. The coordinator hired to guide the effort was Kathaleen Shaw, who has gone on to other posts involving revitalization and is currently with the Keyport Partnership, Inc.

Starting in 1989, Keyport became a place of choice for go-go bars. It was a permitted use in the highway commercial zone, but a go-go bar named Knockers opened on West Front Street by Matawan Creek. The borough took the owners to court and the go-go went. In the same time period, another go-go bar named the Body Shop opened in the highway commercial zone near the Hazlet border. It is still there. In March 1992, an adult bookstore tried to open next to the Body Shop, but it ran into a storm of protest. After reversal of the building permit by the zoning board, a fire set by an arsonist, and court actions

The Strand Theater (formerly the Surf) became an X-rated movie house by the late 1960s and created headlines and court cases.

that extended to October 1997, the would-be proprietors abandoned their plans in January 1998.

Mosquitoes hit the headlines in 1991 and 1992 with the clearing of debris in Chingarora Creek and near Matawan Creek and spraying by the Monmouth County Mosquito Extermination Commission. There were 24 varieties of mosquito found in the bayshore area. In August 1995, the Mosquito Commission identified a 25th variety: the Asian tiger mosquito. Keyport had the dubious honor of being the first place to find it north of the Delaware. In Asia, it is the carrier of the dengue virus.

In March 1992, Mustafa Kilic, owner of the Cornucopia Restaurant, proposed docking a dinner boat on the Keyport waterfront. The borough and Sultan Pier Corporation signed a lease for a large portion of the waterfront for 30 years. Opponents charged that $6,010 per year was too little rent when compared with the higher taxes restaurants in the area were paying, especially when public parking on the waterfront would be part of the package. Proponents felt that it would be good publicity for Keyport and good for the business district. Corps of Engineers and Department of Environmental Protection permits held up approval to proceed. In December 1998, the dinner boat was moved permanently to Perth Amboy.

In 1992, business owners proposed setting up a Special Improvement District, as an offshoot of the Neighborhood Preservation Program, to promote Keyport business. The concept was for businesses in Keyport to pay an extra

Frank Miele retired from the New Jersey State Police and became Keyport's first and only Police Director. The photograph shows him in a procession for his graduating class of 1957.

tax to be collected by the borough and held in a special fund for promotion purposes. Some business owners objected to any additional tax and the need for such a district. After much discussion over several years, the mayor and council created a Business Improvement District (BID) in December 1999. The ordinance called for a board of directors from among the business owners and a tax of 25¢ per $100 of property evaluation. Since then, there have been several special events and several advertising promotions sponsored by BID.

In May 1995, Mayor Kevin Graham announced that Timpano Productions would come to Keyport to film a movie called *Big Night*. Filming began one month later, centering in a transformed lower Broad Street—storefronts there became a barber shop, a florist, and two rival restaurants, with a board fence masking the Stitch property. Crowds assembled to watch the proceedings; a night scene was filmed in front of a redecorated 100 Main Street; period cars were assembled such as Robert Lohsen's black Chevrolet. The movie told of two Italian brothers who fight for the existence of their restaurant against a larger Italian restaurant willing to be less exacting about the traditional dishes served. The film won an award at the Sundance Film Festival but generally bombed at the box office.

In February 1996, Keyport had about six antique shops; by December, there were 16. People were talking about Keyport as Red Bank's rival for the antique business. In March 1997, Newberry's five and ten closed and was replaced by an antiques mall with seemingly countless upscale shops. It appeared that Keyport had arrived. Then in October 1999, the county announced that Keyport's

Front Street bridge over Lupatatong Creek would be replaced and closed the street. The construction continued through May 2000, and businesses in town suffered, many of them closing. Keyport's business section had had a setback.

There had been no ferry service in Keyport since 1990. In December 1999, New York Fast Ferry proposed service between Keyport and New York. Green Acres approval was needed because they had funded the building of the Keyport waterfront. In addition, details had to be worked out concerning parking, docking, and traffic. Ferries at this point were running from Highlands and Atlantic Highlands and a ferry terminal was under construction from Belford. Fast Ferry purchased land on Beers and Front Streets, just a short walk from their proposed dock. In May 2000, Fast Ferry had a demonstration run for borough officials and residents from their dock in Highlands. Merchants in the business section generally felt that ferry service would provide the assistance needed to overcome business losses sustained from the closed Front Street bridge. Keyport held a special town meeting in July for Fast Ferry to speak to the people of Keyport. The response was overwhelmingly in favor of the service.

In the wake of the terrorist attacks on September 11, all approvals for the ferry service were expedited and service started on October 15. They did a very brisk business, but had problems with continuation of the leases for boats by March 2002 and had to reduce the quality of service by leasing fishing boats. After the 9-11 attack, there was a large increase in demand for boats. Fast Ferry had ordered a new boat, the *Christopher Colasanti*, being built in Alabama. In April, the company reported an operational loss of $42.9 million on revenue of $4.4 million the previous year but remained upbeat. By July, it had lost 70 percent of its riders. The new ferry ordered by Fast Ferry arrived in Keyport in October and then sailed away. In the meantime, New York Waterways started service from nearby Belford at facilities built by Monmouth County and were drawing off ridership; they even provided free ridership for their first week. All service by Fast Ferry stopped without notice in November 2002. A major financial backer withdrew, making purchase of the *Christopher Colasanti* an impossibility. Fast Ferry's parent company filed for chapter 11 bankruptcy protection in March 2003.

Through the 1990s and beyond, an interesting project has been ongoing in Sherry Hill's third grade classes. Each year they form Pot Holders R Us Corporation, assign presidents, vice presidents, stockholders, suppliers, people in charge of packaging and of advertising, and people to run inventories. Then they weave pot holders and sell them. The proceeds are donated to a charity. The lessons in business organization and operation are priceless.

By 1999, the bulkhead containing the Keyport waterfront had deteriorated seriously. In September 1999, the state promised Keyport partial funding to replace the bulkhead. An appointed citizens committee with the borough engineer formulated a plan to use heavy fiberglass bulkheading, move American Legion Drive in from the edge, probably making it an extension of First Street, and establish a raised pedestrian walk along the bulkhead. Several approvals are required for such a project, primarily by Green Acres and the Corps of Engineers. Plans and discussions have gone back and forth from 1999 to 2003, but resolution still eludes the borough. Mayor John Merla arranged to bring all parties together to move matters ahead, and a major follow-up meeting is scheduled for August 2003.

Keyport's latest asset is a fire museum at the Broad Street site of the original Raritan Hose Company made possible by a state grant. There are ongoing plans to change the zoning of the business district to also permit residential use. There are also plans to put the Keyport water system up for sale. Additional history is constantly being created. To quote Omar Khayyam, "The moving finger writes, and having writ moves on."

Big Night *was filmed in Keyport. Building faces were transformed for the purpose. The photograph shown is of Pascal's, the successful restaurant in the movie.*

Bibliography

Aeroplane Monthly, 1980.

Asbury Park Press, 1973–2003.

Astaire, Fred. *Steps in Time*. New York: Harper & Brothers, 1959.

Brown, Josephine. Collection at Monmouth County Historical Association, Freehold, NJ.

Bruno, Harry. *Wings Over America*. Garden City, NY: Halcyon House, 1944.

Business History Review, Summer 1979, Harvard School of Business Administration, Cambridge, MA.

Independent, 1973–2003

Interviews:

- Amerling, Robert, 1997
- Baker, David, 1996
- Conklin, Meta, 1983
- Huylar, Wilbur, 1989
- Johnson, William, 1980
- Kneute, Harry, 1994
- Schanck, J. Leon Jr., 1989
- Slovenz, Anita, 1995
- Waterman, Lillian, 1985

Keyport Weekly, 1869–1973.

Klemin, Alexander. "Plant of the Aeromarine Plane & Motor Company." *Aviation*. 7 February 1921.

Loening, Grover. *Take Off Into Greatness*. New York: G.P. Putnam & Sons, 1968.

MacKenzie, Clyde. note December 12, 1989.

Manufacturers Aircraft Association, Aircraft Yearbook, 1920 (New York, 1920); Uppercu testimony, December 11, 1919, U.S. House of Representatives, United Air Service; Hearing Before a Subcommittee of the Committee on Military Affairs 66th Congress, 2nd Session (Washington, D.C., 1921) Pg 335.

Monmouth County Wills, Inventories, etc., Hall of Records, Freehold, New Jersey.

Newspapers, local, Monmouth County, mid-1800s:

- *Democratic Banner*
- *Inquirer*

N.J. Standard
Olive Branch
Union
New York Globe, November 1910.
Reichers, Lou. *The Flying Years*. New York: Henry Holt & Company, 1956.
Reilly, H.V. Pat. *From the Balloon to the Moon*. Oradell, NJ: HV Publishers, 1992.
Reusille, Leon. *Steam Vessels Built in Old Monmouth*. Brick Township, NJ: J.I. Farley Printing, 1975.
Sinclair, Andrew. *Prohibition—The Era of Excess*. Boston: Little Brown & Company, 1962.
Willoughby, Malcolm F. *Rum War at Sea*. Washington D.C.: Government Printing Office, 1964.
Zimmerman, Cy. *The Log of an Aeromarine*. Keyport, NJ: Aeromarine Plane & Motor Company, 1920.

Firemen parading past the steamboat docks in 1927 celebrating their 50th anniversary.

INDEX

Arthur Rooke, Superintendent of Public Works for many years.